Activists, Rebels, and Reformers

Activists, Rebels, and Reformers

Volume 1: A-F

PHILLIS ENGELBERT

Diane Sawinski, Editor

AN IMPRINT OF THE GALE GROUP

DETROIT · NEW YORK · SAN FRANCISCO
LONDON · BOSTON · WOODBRIDGE, CT

Phillis Engelbert

Staff

Diane Sawinski, *U·X·L Senior Editor*
Stacy McConnell and Gerda-Ann Raffaelle, *U·X·L Editors*
Carol DeKane Nagel, *U·X·L Managing Editor*
Thomas L. Romig, *U·X·L Publisher*

Sarah Tomasek, *Permissions Specialist*
Renee McPhail, *Research Assistant to Author*

Dean Dauphinais, *Senior Editor, Imaging and Multimedia Content*
Pamela A. Reed, *Imaging Coordinator*
Robert Duncan, *Imaging Specialist*
Randy Bassett, *Imaging Supervisor*
Barbara J. Yarrow, *Manager, Imaging and Multimedia Content*

Pamela A. E. Galbreath, *Senior Art Director*
Kenn Zorn, *Product Design Manager*

Rita Wimberley, *Senior Buyer*
Dorothy Maki, *Manufacturing Manager*
Evi Seoud, *Assistant Manager, Composition Purchasing and Electronic Prepress*
Mary Beth Trimper, *Manager, Composition and Electronic Prepress*

Linda Mahoney, LM Design, *Typesetting*

Cover photograph of Rigoberta Menchú (with megaphone) reproduced by permission of AP/Wide World Photos. Cover photographs of Mary Harris "Mother" Jones and Frederick Douglass reproduced by permission of the Library of Congress.

Library of Congress Cataloging-in-Publication Data

Engelbert, Phillis.

  Activists, rebels, & reformers / Phillis Engelbert ; Diane Sawinski, editor.

    p. cm.

  Includes bibliographical references and index.

  ISBN 0-7876-4847-7 (set) — ISBN 0-7876-4848-5 (vol. 1) - ISBN 0-7876-4849-3 (vol. 2) —ISBN 0-7876-4850-7 (vol. 3)

  1. Social reformers—Biography—Juvenile literature. 2. Political activists—Biography—Juvenile literature. 3. Dissenters—Biography—Juvenile literature. [1. Reformers. 2. Political activists. 3. Dissenters.] I. Title: Activists, rebels, and reformers. II. Sawinski, Diane M. III. Title.

HN17.5 .E534 2000
303.48′4′0922—dc21
[B]   00-34365

Printed in the United States of America
10 9 8 7 6 5 4 3 2 1

Contents

Volume 2: G–M

Volume 3: N–Z

Activists by Cause

Italic numerals indicate volume numbers.

Reader's Guide

Activists, Rebels, and Reformers contains biographical sketches of sixty-eight individuals plus seven organizations that have helped shape the course of history. Prominent movers and shakers are covered, as well as lesser-known agitators, from a variety of times and places.

Activists and organizations featured include: Jane Addams, who fought for peace and the rights of women and poor immigrant workers in Chicago at the turn of the twentieth century; Amnesty International, an organization dedicated to upholding human rights around the world and freeing all "prisoners of conscience"; Mohandas Gandhi, who united the citizens of India to peacefully overthrow British rule in the 1940s; and Nelson Mandela, who guided South Africa through a relatively peaceful transition to a multiracial democracy in the 1990s after having spent twenty-five years as a political prisoner. The essays are intended to inform and inspire students, as well as to empower them with the knowledge that ordinary people can make a difference in community and world affairs.

Format

Activists, Rebels, and Reformers is arranged in alphabetical order over three volumes. Each biography is five to ten pages long. Sidebars containing short biographies of associated individuals, descriptions of writings by or about the person or organization in the entry, and other relevant and interesting information highlight the text. More than 120 photographs and illustrations help bring the subject matter to life. Difficult words are defined, cross-references to related entries are made within the text, and a further readings section accompanies each entry. Each volume concludes with a cumulative subject index, providing easy access to the people and movements discussed throughout *Activists, Rebels, and Reformers*.

Special thanks

The author offers most special thanks to Renee McPhail—research czarina, manuscript reader, and extraordinarily good friend. Appreciation is also due to U•X•L editors Diane Sawinski and Gerda-Ann Raffaelle for coordinating the final stages of this project; to University of Michigan Spanish professor Eliana Moya-Raggio and economist Dean Baker of the Washington, D.C.-based Center for Economic and Policy Research for their assistance with select entries; and to the following scholars and activists who suggested entries for inclusion: Rev. Joseph Summers, Ted Sylvester, Ingrid Kock, Kidada Williams, Susan Tachna, and Matt Calvert. Finally, sincere thanks go to Bill Shea and Ryan Patrick Shea—the best husband and son an author could hope for.

Comments and suggestions

We welcome your comments on *Activists, Rebels, and Reformers* as well as your suggestions for entries to be included in future volumes. Please write: Editors, *Activists, Rebels, and Reformers* U•X•L, 27500 Drake Rd., Farmington Hills, MI 48331–3535; call toll-free 1–800–877–4253; fax to 248–699–8097; or send e-mail via http://www.galegroup.com.

Advisory Board

Special thanks are due for the invaluable comments and suggestions provided by U•X•L's *Activists, Rebels, and Reformers* advisors:

- Tracey Easthope, Director of Environmental Health Project, Ecology Center, Ann Arbor, Michigan

- Frances Hasso, Assistant Professor of Sociology and Women's Studies, Oberlin College, Oberlin, Ohio

- Elizabeth James, Librarian, Center for Afroamerican and African Studies, University of Michigan, Ann Arbor, Michigan

- Premilla Nadasen, Assistant Professor of African-American History, Queens College, New York, New York

- Jan Toth-Chernin, Media Specialist, Greenhills School, Ann Arbor, Michigan

Timeline of Events

1818   English Quaker prison reformer **Elizabeth Fry** founds the British Ladies' Society for Promoting the Reformation of Female Prisoners.

1837   Abolitionists **Sarah and Angelina Grimké** undertake a speaking tour of New York State on behalf of the American Anti-Slavery Society.

1837   Attorney and politician **Horace Mann** successfully campaigns to establish a Massachusetts State Board of Education and becomes the board's first secretary. In that position he reforms the state's public school system, making it a model for the rest of the nation.

1847   **Frederick Douglass** begins publishing the antislavery paper *North Star* in Rochester, New York.

1800	1825	1844
The Library of Congress is established	J. N. Niepce creates the first permanent photograph	Samuel Morse sends the first telegraph message

1800	1815	1830	1845

1848   **Karl Marx** and Friedrich Engels publish *The Communist Manifesto,* calling on working people to overthrow their governments and establish a communist society.

1848   Women's rights convention is held at Seneca Falls, New York, to discuss women's suffrage and the abolition of slavery.

1850   **Harriet Tubman** makes her first of many journeys into the South to help slaves escape to freedom.

1850   Congress enacts the Fugitive Slave Act, which requires federal marshals to arrest any black person accused of being a runaway slave. This legislation results in the return to the South, and slavery, of many escaped slaves and free blacks in the North and intensifies the battle over slavery.

October 16, 1859   **John Brown** leads a group of twenty-one men on a failed raid of Harpers Ferry armory in Virginia in an attempt to spark an armed rebellion of slaves against their masters.

1865   Slavery is abolished with the passage of the Thirteenth Amendment.

1869   Suffragists **Elizabeth Cady Stanton** and Susan B. Anthony found the National Woman Suffrage Association (NWSA) to press for a constitutional amendment guaranteeing women the right to vote.

1886   Striking workers at Chicago's McCormick Harvesting Machine Company hold a rally in Haymarket Square. Seven police officers are killed by a dynamite bomb detonated at the rally, a crime for which eight union leaders are later convicted despite a lack of evidence. Four of those convicted are eventually hanged.

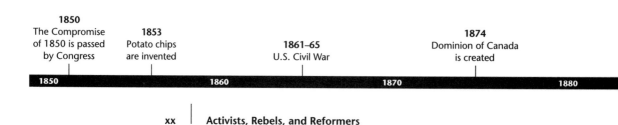

1850
The Compromise
of 1850 is passed
by Congress

1853
Potato chips
are invented

1861–65
U.S. Civil War

1874
Dominion of Canada
is created

1850   1860   1870   1880

1889   Social reformers **Jane Addams** and Ellen G. Starr inaugurate the community center and welfare agency called Hull House in Chicago.

1890   U.S. forces massacre between 150 and 370 Native Americans at Wounded Knee in South Dakota.

1890   The National American Woman Suffrage Association (NAWSA) is formed by the merger of two rival suffrage organizations: the National Woman Suffrage Association and the American Woman Suffrage Association.

1903   Labor leader **Mary Harris "Mother" Jones** leads thousands of youthful textile workers on a 125–mile march from Philadelphia to the New York home of President Theodore Roosevelt to protest child labor.

1911   Mexican revolutionary **Emiliano Zapata** issues his revolutionary manifesto, the *Plan de Alaya*, which advocates the overthrow of the government, the forcible repossession of lands stolen from farmers, and the redistribution of one-third of all plantation lands to peasants.

1912   Workplace safety advocate **Florence Kelley** successfully lobbies for the formation of the United States Children's Bureau, the nation's first child welfare agency.

1913   Feminists **Alice Paul** and Lucy Burns found the radical suffrage organization Congressional Union, which in 1917 becomes part of the National Woman's Party.

1915   Legendary labor leader **Joe Hill** is executed by firing squad in Utah for the alleged murders of a grocery store owner and his son.

1917   **American Friends Service Committee** is founded in Philadelphia to help conscientious objectors (people

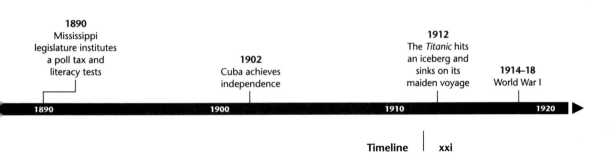

1890
Mississippi
legislature institutes
a poll tax and
literacy tests

1902
Cuba achieves
independence

1912
The *Titanic* hits
an iceberg and
sinks on its
maiden voyage

1914–18
World War I

1890   1900   1910   1920

opposed to serving in wars) find alternative ways to serve the global community.

1917 The United States enters World War I (1914–18).

January 1919 Polish revolutionary political leader **Rosa Luxemburg** leads a failed worker rebellion in Berlin, Germany. She is captured and killed by the army.

March 1919 Journalist/activist **John Reed** publishes *Ten Days That Shook the World,* which wins acclaim as the finest eyewitness account of the Russian revolution.

April 1919 Mexican revolutionary **Emiliano Zapata** is assassinated by enemy troops.

December 1919 Russian-American Jewish anarchist **Emma Goldman** is expelled from the United States for her activities protesting U.S. involvement in World War I.

1920 The Nineteenth Amendment is passed, granting women the right to vote.

1925 **A. Philip Randolph** founds the Brotherhood of Sleeping Car Porters, the first black labor union in the United States.

1927–33 Rebel leader **Augusto Cesar Sandino** and his band of guerrilla fighters challenge the U.S. Marines for control of Nicaragua.

1930 **Mohandas Gandhi** leads his fellow Indians on a 240-mile "salt march" to the sea in defiance of British authorities.

1931 **Jane Addams** is awarded the Nobel Peace Prize.

1932 Educator and civil rights activist Myles Horton founds the **Highlander Research and Education Center**, the South's only integrated educational institution at the

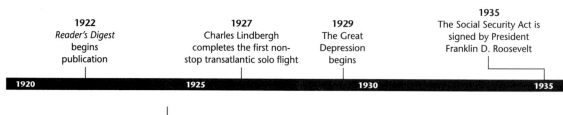

1922
Reader's Digest begins publication

1927
Charles Lindbergh completes the first non-stop transatlantic solo flight

1929
The Great Depression begins

1935
The Social Security Act is signed by President Franklin D. Roosevelt

1920   1925   1930   1935

| Activists, Rebels, and Reformers

time, in the Appalachian Mountains near Monteagle, Tennessee.

1935 Peace activist **Dorothy Day** founds the Catholic worker movement in New York.

1940 **Saul Alinsky**, a self-described "professional radical" from Chicago, founds the Industrial Areas Foundation for the training of community organizers.

1947 India achieves independence from Great Britain.

1950 Civil rights activist and performer **Paul Robeson**'s passport is revoked by the U.S. State Department and he is blacklisted by entertainment industry officials for his alleged communist sympathies.

1950 Civil rights activist and educator **Jo Ann Gibson Robinson** takes over as president of the Women's Political Committee (WPC). Under her leadership, the WPC lays the groundwork for the 1955–56 boycott of city buses by African Americans in Montgomery, Alabama.

1954 The Supreme Court, in *Brown v. Board of Education,* declares school segregation unconstitutional.

1955–56 Black residents of Montgomery, Alabama, stage a boycott of city buses, resulting in the racial integration of the buses.

1956 Civil rights activist **Robert F. Williams** takes over the Monroe, North Carolina, chapter of the National Association for the Advancement of Colored People (NAACP; founded in 1909) and arms its members so they can defend local African Americans against the Ku Klux Klan.

1957 Ghana becomes the first African nation to achieve independence from a colonial power and **Kwame Nkrumah** is named its first prime minister.

1939–45
World War II

1944
The United Nations establishes the International Bank for Reconstruction (World Bank) and the International Monetary Fund

1950
Comic strip "Peanuts" by *St. Paul Pioneer Press* cartoonist Charles Schulz debuts in eight newspapers

1954–75
Vietnam War

1940   1945   1950   1955

1959 U.S.-backed dictator Fulgencia Batista flees Cuba; Fidel Castro and **Ernesto "Ché" Guevara** lead triumphant rebel troops through the streets of Havana.

1960 The **Student Nonviolent Coordinating Committee** is founded in Raleigh, North Carolina.

1961 Medical doctor and revolutionary **Frantz Fanon** publishes *The Wretched of the Earth*, in which he advocates that colonized people violently overthrow their oppressors.

1961 **Amnesty International** is founded in England by lawyer Peter Benenson with the mission of freeing all "prisoners of conscience."

1962 Peace activist **Tom Hayden** authors "The Port Huron Statement," the political treatise defining the mission of the **Students for a Democratic Society.** The essay calls the American political establishment morally bankrupt and oppressive, and condemns militarism, materialism, and cultural conformity.

1962 Radical civil rights activist **Gloria Richardson** becomes cochair of the Cambridge Nonviolent Action Committee (CNAC). CNAC stages a militant, prolonged fight for the rights of African Americans in Cambridge, Maryland.

May 1963 Young activists of the "children's crusade" march for civil rights in Birmingham, Alabama, and are brutalized by the police.

August 1963 More than 250,000 people participate in the March on Washington for Jobs and Freedom. **Martin Luther King, Jr.**, delivers his "I Have a Dream" speech.

March 1964 Malcolm X forms the black nationalist group Organization of Afro-American Unity (OAAU).

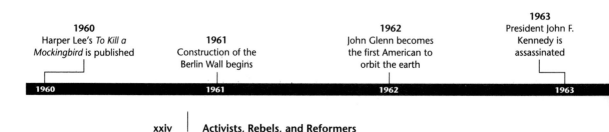

1960
Harper Lee's *To Kill a Mockingbird* is published

1961
Construction of the Berlin Wall begins

1962
John Glenn becomes the first American to orbit the earth

1963
President John F. Kennedy is assassinated

1960   1961   1962   1963

June 1964 One-thousand college-student volunteers descend on Mississippi for the beginning of Freedom Summer. They register voters, run freedom schools, and organize the Mississippi Freedom Democratic Party.

July 1964 President Lyndon B. Johnson signs the Civil Rights Act, thereby outlawing a variety of types of discrimination based on race, color, religion, or national origin.

October 1964 Student activist **Mario Savio** leads the Free Speech Movement on the campus of the University of California at Berkeley.

1965 The National Farm Workers Association, which changes its named to United Farm Workers in April 1966, is founded in Delano, California.

1965 Native American groups in the Pacific Northwest hold "fish-ins" to protest unconstitutional restrictions placed upon their fishing rights by state governments.

1965 Consumer advocate **Ralph Nader** publishes *Unsafe at Any Speed,* in which he criticizes General Motors for marketing the Corvair and other cars that he alleges the company knows to be unsafe.

February 21, 1965 **Malcolm** X is assassinated in Harlem, New York.

August 6, 1965 President Lyndon B. Johnson signs the Voting Rights Act, thereby outlawing all practices used to deny blacks the right to vote and empowering federal registrars to register black voters.

1966 The **Black Panther Party** is founded in Oakland, California.

October 1967 Countercultural activist **Abbie Hoffman** leads 75,000 people in a mass "exorcism of demons" at the

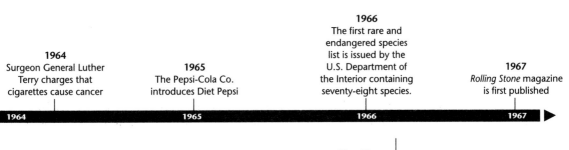

1964
Surgeon General Luther Terry charges that cigarettes cause cancer

1965
The Pepsi-Cola Co. introduces Diet Pepsi

1966
The first rare and endangered species list is issued by the U.S. Department of the Interior containing seventy-eight species.

1967
Rolling Stone magazine is first published

1964   1965   1966   1967

Pentagon in Washington, D.C., in protest of the Vietnam War (1954–75).

April 4, 1968 Martin Luther King, Jr., is assassinated in Memphis, Tennessee.

May 1968 Student activist **Daniel Cohn-Bendit** leads French students in a nationwide revolt.

May 1968 Daniel and Philip Berrigan and seven other peace activists use napalm to burn draft records at the Selective Service office in Catonsville, Maryland, in protest of the Vietnam War (1954–75).

July 1968 The **American Indian Movement** is founded in Minneapolis, Minnesota.

August 1968 Thousands of antiwar and antiracism protesters converge on the Democratic National Convention in Chicago. In what is later described as a "police riot," columns of police beat and tear-gas nonviolent demonstrators.

November 1969–June 1971 Indians of All Tribes occupies Alcatraz Island, San Francisco Bay, California, demanding it be returned to Native Americans.

December 4, 1969 Black Panther Party activists Fred Hampton and Mark Clark are shot to death by police in a predawn raid on their Chicago apartment.

1970 Brazilian educator **Paulo Freire** publishes his most famous book, *Pedagogy of the Oppressed,* in which he outlines a teaching method for illiterate adults that encourages them to participate in the transformation of the society in which they live.

1971 Environmental scientist **Barry Commoner** publishes his best-selling book, *The Closing Circle,* in which he

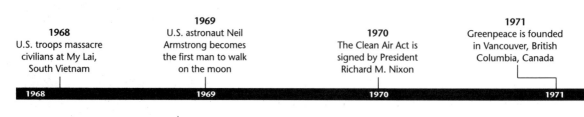

1968
U.S. troops massacre civilians at My Lai, South Vietnam

1969
U.S. astronaut Neil Armstrong becomes the first man to walk on the moon

1970
The Clean Air Act is signed by President Richard M. Nixon

1971
Greenpeace is founded in Vancouver, British Columbia, Canada

1968   1969   1970   1971

argues that technology has the potential to destroy human society.

1971 **Jesse Jackson** founds PUSH (People United to Serve Humanity) in Chicago.

June 1972 Radical activist **Angela Davis,** in one of the most closely watched trials in history, is acquitted of charges of kidnapping, conspiracy, and murder in connection with the attempted escape of a prisoner in California.

1972–73 Members of the **American Indian Movement** and other Native Americans occupy the village of Wounded Knee on the Pine Ridge Reservation in South Dakota in protest of the corrupt tribal government of chairman Dick Wilson.

1975 Mozambique wins independence from Portugal; **Samora Machel** becomes the new republic's first president.

1976 **Mairead Corrigan and Betty Williams** win the Nobel Peace Prize for their efforts to bring about peace in war-torn Northern Ireland.

1976 Civil rights activist **Unita Blackwell** is elected mayor of Mayersville, Mississippi, a town that had previously denied her the right to vote.

1978 **Lois Gibbs** becomes president of the Love Canal (New York) Homeowners Association, a group organized to fight for the cleanup of hazardous wastes that had been dumped at the site by Hooker Chemical Company in the 1940s.

July 1979 The Sandinista Front for National Liberation (known by the Spanish acronym FSLN, or Sandinistas) topples the U.S.-backed dictatorship in Nicaragua.

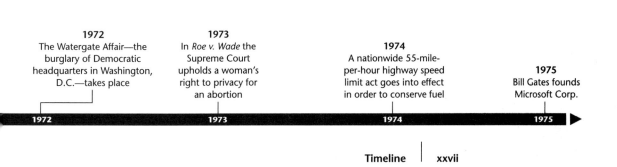

1972
The Watergate Affair—the burglary of Democratic headquarters in Washington, D.C.—takes place

1973
In *Roe v. Wade* the Supreme Court upholds a woman's right to privacy for an abortion

1974
A nationwide 55-mile-per-hour highway speed limit act goes into effect in order to conserve fuel

1975
Bill Gates founds Microsoft Corp.

1972   1973   1974   1975

March 24, 1980 Archbishop **Oscar Romero** of El Salvador, an outspoken critic of the violence committed by the armed forces in his country, is assassinated as he conducts mass.

1982 Egyptian feminist **Nawal El Saadawi** founds the Arab Women's Solidarity Association (AWSA), an international group of Arab women committed to "lifting the veil from the mind" of women.

1982 **Tom Hayden** is elected to the California State Assembly. He serves until 1991, at which time he is elected to the state senate. California's term limit law forced him to give up his state senate seat in 1999.

1983 The Women's Encampment for a Future of Peace and Justice protests nuclear arms at the Seneca Army Depot in Romulus, New York.

1985 The Indigenous Women's Network is founded by women representing three hundred Indian nations at a five-day conference at the Yelm, Washington, home of **Janet McCloud.**

1986 Native American activist **Winona LaDuke** founds the White Earth Land Recovery Project, the goal of which is to buy back or otherwise reclaim former Indian lands.

1988 Indigenous Malaysian **Harrison Ngau** is granted the Right Livelihood Award (considered the alternative Nobel Peace Prize) for his efforts to stop logging in the rainforest of Borneo.

1989 Radical feminist and author **Margaret Randall**'s U.S. citizenship is restored by the Immigration Appeals Board. The Immigration and Naturalization Service had denied Randall's citizenship and tried to deport her from the country in 1985 because her writings

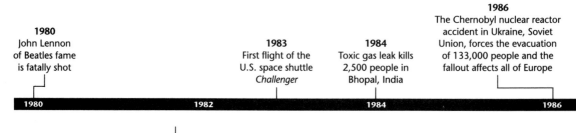

1980
John Lennon of Beatles fame is fatally shot

1983
First flight of the U.S. space shuttle *Challenger*

1984
Toxic gas leak kills 2,500 people in Bhopal, India

1986
The Chernobyl nuclear reactor accident in Ukraine, Soviet Union, forces the evacuation of 133,000 people and the fallout affects all of Europe

| 1980 | 1982 | 1984 | 1986 |

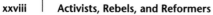

were deemed to "advocate the economic, international and governmental doctrines of world communism."

1990 Israeli lawyer **Felicia Langer** quits her practice of defending Palestinian victims of human rights abuses and leaves the country, stating that justice for Palestinians is impossible in the Israeli military court system.

May 1990 A bomb explodes in the car of environmental activists **Judi Bari** and Darryl Cherney as they drive to a college campus to recruit volunteers for Redwood Summer (a summer-long demonstration against the logging of ancient redwoods). Bari is seriously injured; the case remains unsolved.

1991 **Aung San Suu Kyi** is awarded the Nobel Peace Prize for her efforts to bring democracy to Myanmar (Burma).

1991 **Patricia Ireland** takes over as president of the National Organization for Women (NOW).

1992 **Rigoberta Menchú** receives the Nobel Peace Prize for her work on behalf of social, political, and economic justice for Guatemalan Indians.

1992 Chinese émigré and former political prisoner **Harry Wu** founds the Laogai Foundation in the United States to educate Americans about human rights abuses in China and to advocate for reform.

1993 **Nelson Mandela** and South African President F. W. deKlerk are jointly awarded the Nobel Peace Prize for leading their nation down a nonviolent path toward democracy.

1993 Bangladeshi writer **Taslima Nasrin**'s first novel, *Shame,* is published, leading to calls for her death by Muslim fundamentalists.

1988
Internet virus jams over six thousand military computers

1989
Demolition of the Berlin Wall begins

1991
Operation Desert Storm to end the Persian Gulf War is launched

1994
Major League baseball players strike forces the cancellation of the World Series

1988　　　　　　1990　　　　　1992　　　　　1994

1994 **Nelson Mandela** wins the presidency of South Africa in the country's first all-race elections.

1996 The passage of Proposition 209 in California ends that state's policy of affirmative action in government agencies.

1996 **Ralph Nader** and **Winona LaDuke** run for president and vice-president of the United States on the Green Party ticket. (Nader runs again in 2000.)

1997 Chinese pro-democracy activist **Wei Jingsheng** is freed and sent to the United States after spending seventeen years in prison in his native country.

March 4, 1999 Native American activist **Ingrid Washinawa-tok**, in Colombia to assist the U'wa people in their fight against oil drilling on their land, is killed by rebel soldiers.

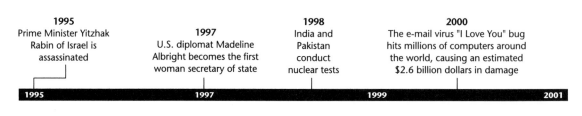

1995
Prime Minister Yitzhak Rabin of Israel is assassinated

1997
U.S. diplomat Madeline Albright becomes the first woman secretary of state

1998
India and Pakistan conduct nuclear tests

2000
The e-mail virus "I Love You" bug hits millions of computers around the world, causing an estimated $2.6 billion dollars in damage

1995   1997   1999   2001

Activists, Rebels, and Reformers

Jane Addams

Born September 6, 1860
Cedarville, Illinois
Died May 21, 1935
Chicago, Illinois

Founder of Hull House and the Women's
International League for Peace and Freedom

Jane Addams came from a wealthy, influential family and chose to live among and advocate for the poor. Originally committed to performing charity work, Addams later recognized that the road to equality lay in extensive social reform. To that end, she founded and spent forty years at Hull House, a community center, neighborhood association, and cultural and educational institution in a working-class section of Chicago, Illinois. Addams advocated that women have career opportunities and the right to vote. She also brought together women in the United States and Europe to work for world peace. She received the Nobel Peace Prize in 1931.

Upbringing in a prominent family

Jane Addams was born in Cedarville, a farming community in northern Illinois, on September 6, 1860. She was the youngest of five surviving children (three others died in infancy and one died at age sixteen). Hers was the wealthiest and most influential family in the community. When Addams was two years old, her mother, Sarah Weber, died during childbirth. Her father, John Huy Addams, married Anna H. Halderman six years later.

"We early learned to know the children of hard driven mothers who went out to work all day, sometimes leaving the little things in the casual care of a neighbor, but often locking them into their tenement rooms."

Jane Addams in Twenty Years at Hull House

Jane Addams.
Courtesy of the Library of Congress.

Addams's main influence during her childhood was her father. John Addams was prominent in the areas of politics, business, and religion. He was known for his antislavery views, as well as his honesty and integrity. He served in the Illinois state senate for sixteen years (from 1854 to 1870) and assisted future U.S. President Abraham Lincoln (1809–1865; president 1861–65), with whom he had a personal friendship, in the formation of the Republican Party in 1854. Addams financed and trained a Cedarville unit in the Union Army (the army of the northern states during the American Civil War [1861–1865]) and served as an officer in the unit. He founded a grain mill and a lumber mill in his community and was a bank president. He also established the community's school, library, insurance company, and church (where he taught Sunday school classes).

Jane Addams's father and stepmother instilled in her the ideals of individual rights, equal opportunity, Christian ethics, and community responsibility. Addams was taught that it was her role, as a member of a democracy, to seek solutions to social problems.

Blazes trail in women's education

Women of Addams's generation were some of the first in the United States to have the opportunity to attend college. Prior to the late 1870s, higher education was believed to interfere with women's childbearing capabilities. Addams' first choice for college was Smith, in Northampton, Massachusetts, then considered to be the best women's college in the United States. But Addams succumbed to pressure from her father to stay close to home and enrolled in the Rockford Female Seminary in Illinois. The goal of Rockford was to educate women in order to make them better wives and mothers or for careers as teachers or missionaries.

Addams attended Rockford from 1877 to 1881. She was president of her class each of the four years, editor of the school newspaper, president of the literary society, and valedictorian. The school gained accreditation as a college in 1882, at which time Addams was awarded a bachelor's degree.

Addams's experience in college solidified her desire for a career in community service. She set her sights on becoming a doctor, so she could work in poor areas. Disobeying the wishes of her family (it was expected in that era that the youngest daughter would remain at home to care for her parents as they aged), she enrolled in the Women's Medical College in Philadelphia, Pennsylvania.

During her first year of medical school, however, Addams suffered a series of illnesses. She was diagnosed with "vertebrae problems" and "nervous exhaustion." Addams dropped out of school and entered a hospital for treatment.

Travels abroad

From 1883 to 1885 Addams toured and studied in Europe. Addams then returned to Illinois and spent two years reading, writing, and thinking about her future. During that period she studied the social philosophy of John Ruskin (1819–1900), the English author and painter who linked capitalism with social injustice.

In 1887 Addams convinced her friend from Rockford, Ellen G. Starr, to accompany her on a second trip to Europe. The highlight of their tour was in England when they visited Toynbee Hall, a settlement house in London's industrial East End (that served as a social reform and social welfare center; see box). There university students worked with Christian social reformers to alleviate urban poverty. That visit inspired Addams to open a similar settlement house in Chicago.

Founds Hull House

Upon their return from Europe, Addams and Starr opened a settlement house in a run-down mansion in Chicago. They inaugurated Hull House named for Charles Hull, who built the house in the 1850s, on September 8, 1889. The mansion was located at the corner of Halsted and Polk Streets, which at that time was a poor area (it is now an affluent section of Chicago). The neighborhood was inhabited primarily by immigrants and other people who had been drawn to the city by the promise of industrial jobs but whose wages were barely sufficient to cover their basic needs. Like immigrants in New York, Boston, and other urban areas during that time period, Chicago immigrants lived in dirty, crowded conditions.

The Settlement House Movement

A settlement house (also called social settlement, community center, neighborhood house, or neighborhood social welfare agency) is an organization devoted to the improvement of neighborhood life. Settlement houses offer a variety of services, such as youth clubs, child care, athletic teams, meeting spaces for groups, counseling, and educational programs. Social workers and activists live in the settlement house, thus immersing themselves in the daily rhythms and existing problems of the neighborhood.

The settlement house movement began with the establishment of Toynbee Hall in London, England, in 1884. The first settlement house in the United States was Neighborhood Guild (later renamed University Settlement), opened in 1886 on New York City's Lower East Side. Jane Addams initiated the nation's most famous settlement house, Hull House, on the West Side of Chicago in 1889. In 1891 Andover House (later renamed South End House) was founded in Boston, Massachusetts, by Robert A. Woods, a former staff member of Toynbee Hall. Settlement houses also sprang up throughout western Europe and in Southeast Asia and Japan.

The settlement house movement in the United States was strongest in the late 1800s and early 1900s, when masses of immigrants lived in squalor in urban areas. Some four hundred settlement houses opened in the United States before World War I (1914–18). The year 1926 saw the founding of the International Federation of Settlements and Neighborhood Centers (IFS), headquartered in Utrech, Netherlands. The federation has observer status in the United Nations, meaning it is allowed to observe proceedings and participate in committees.

At present, the IFS has thousands of member organizations. To learn more about the IFS and its member organizations, see the IFS Web site at http://www.ifsderby.demon.co.uk/1index.htm.

Addams initially financed Hull House with her inheritance. Private donations (primarily from wealthy women in Chicago) kept the center going in later years. Addams recruited young women from affluent families to move in to the house and assist with caring for children and sick people. By its second year of existence, Hull House offered kindergarten classes, hot lunches, child care, club meetings for older children, parties, meeting space for unions, and a night school for adults (with instruction in English, art, and history). Some two thousand people took advantage of Hull House's services every week.

Addams eventually acquired thirteen large buildings for Hull House, taking over most of a city block, plus a nature camp near Lake Geneva, Wisconsin. The buildings, which surrounded a playground, housed an art gallery, a public kitchen, a coffee house, a gymnasium, a swimming pool, a boarding house for young working women, a book bindery, an art studio, a music school, a theater, a library, an employment center, and a labor museum.

Reformers gather at Hull House

Hull House attracted the attention of prominent American social reformers, several of whom took up residence there (many others attended meetings there). The circle of activists at Hull House worked for antipoverty measures, the rights of women in the workplace, an end to child labor, the establishment of juvenile protection agencies, safety measures in factories, and the right of women to vote. They also helped with the formation of labor unions.

Among the many activists and intellectuals drawn to Hull House were: Alice Hamilton (1869–1970; medical doctor and workplace safety advocate); John Dewey (1859–1952; philosopher and educational reformer); Myles Horton (1905–1990; civil rights activist and adult educator); Julia Lathrop (1858–1932; advocate for the welfare of children and the mentally ill); and **Florence Kelley** (1859–1932; feminist and advocate for workplace safety and shorter working hours; see entry).

Addams's activities outside of Hull House

Once Hull House operations were running smoothly, Addams extended her energies beyond the agency. She served on the Chicago Board of Education, cofounded the Chicago School of Civics and Philanthropy, and became the first woman president of the National Conference of Charities and Corrections (later renamed the National Conference of Social Work). Addams was also a vice president of the National-American Woman Suffrage Association (a women's voting-rights organization; see **Elizabeth Cady Stanton** entry) and a founding member of the National Association for the Advancement of Colored People.

Addams lobbied the Chicago government to construct parks, playgrounds, kindergartens, and public baths in poor neighborhoods. She also worked with social reformers and professors to establish a School of Social Work at the University of Chicago for collecting information about social ills and lobbying for change.

Books, articles, and lectures

In addition to being a full-time social activist, Addams made time to write ten books, hundreds of articles, and thousands of speeches. In her writings Addams argued that a true democracy requires the political and economic empowerment of all citizens. She also denounced war and advocated the negotiated settlement of political problems. Addams argued for the rights of women to vote and to have educational and professional opportunities equal to those of men.

Two of Addams's most popular writings chronicle her career at Hull House. The first, *Twenty Years at Hull House,* was published in 1910; the second, *The Second Twenty Years at Hull House,* was published in 1930. The two books were published in a single volume, *Forty Years at Hull House,* in 1935.

The following excerpt from *Twenty Years at Hull House* provides a description of the type of work carried out at Hull House:

> We early learned to know the children of hard driven mothers who went out to work all day, sometimes leaving the little things in the casual care of a neighbor, but often locking them into their tenement rooms. . . . When the hot weather came the restless children could not brook the confinement of the stuffy rooms, and, as it was not considered safe to leave the doors open because of sneak thieves, many of the children were locked out. During our first summer an increasing number of these poor little mites would wander into the cool hallway of Hull House. We kept them there and fed them at noon. . . .
>
> Hull House was thus committed to a day nursery which we sustained for sixteen years first in a little cottage on a side street and then in a building designed for its use called the Children's House.

Promotes peace during World War I

By the time World War I broke out in 1914, Addams had a long track record as a pacifist (one who advocates peace). She taught a course in peace studies at the University of Wisconsin in the summer of 1906, after which she published a book titled *Newer Ideals of Peace*. Addams gave an address at the 1913 dedication of the Peace Palace in the Hague, Netherlands. In 1914 and 1915 she delivered a series of lectures against American entry into the war (U.S. troops joined the fighting in April 1917).

During World War I (1914–18) Addams served as chair of the Women's Peace Party (an American women's political organization) and as president of the International Congress of Women. The latter organization gave rise to the Women's International League for Peace and Freedom (WILPF), founded in 1919. Addams was named as WILPF's first president. She served in that capacity until 1929, after which she was made honorary president for life.

In the aftermath of World War I, Addams joined a relief effort distributing food to women and children in nations with which the United States had been at war. She chronicled those experiences in her 1922 book *Peace and Bread in Time of War*.

America's love/hate relationship with Jane Addams

Prior to World War I, Addams was one of the most widely respected individuals in the United States. She was called "the only saint America has produced" by British labor leader John Burns (1858–1943) in 1906 (in *American National Biography*). Yale University awarded Addams an honorary doctorate degree in 1910. The *Philadelphia North American* printed in 1912 that Addams was "probably the most widely beloved of her sex in all the world."

With Addams's opposition to the war, however, public and media opinion turned against her. She was labeled a traitor and a subversive (one who seeks to overthrow the government). At least one organization to which she belonged, the Daughters of the American Revolution (a patriotic women's organization), discontinued her membership.

The political tide turned in the late 1920s and Addams regained widespread respect. She was awarded the Nobel Peace Prize in 1931.

Addams suffered a heart attack in 1926, from which she never fully recovered. She was too ill in 1931 to travel to

Oslo, Norway, to deliver the customary acceptance speech for a Nobel Prize. Addams died of cancer on May 21, 1935. Thousands of mourners, from the disadvantaged people she had served to dignitaries, attended her funeral in the courtyard of Hull House.

The demise of Hull House

In 1961 the University of Illinois chose the block occupied by Hull House as the site of its new Chicago campus. University and government officials pressured Hull House trustees to sell most of the buildings. Over the protests of area residents, every Hull House structure except the original Hull House mansion was taken over by the university. Today the mansion serves as a Hull House museum and the headquarters of several nonprofit organizations.

Sources

Books

Addams, Jane. *Forty Years at Hull House*. New York: MacMillan Company, 1935. Contains *Twenty Years at Hull House* and *The Second Twenty Years at Hull House*).

Brown, Victoria Bissell. "Addams, Jane." *American National Biography*. Vol. 1. Edited by John A. Garraty and Mark C. Carnes. New York: Oxford University Press, 1999.

Linn, James W. *Jane Addams: A Biography*. New York: Appleton-Century, 1935.

Tims, Margaret. *Jane Addams of Hull House*. London, England: George Allen & Unwin, Ltd., 1961.

Speeches by Jane Addams

"A Modern Lear." *Survey*. November 2, 1912, pp. 131–37. [Online] Available http://douglass.speech.nwu.edu/adda_a01.htm (accessed November 1, 1999).

"The Subjective Necessity for Social Settlements." *Philanthropy and Social Progress*. New York: Thomas Y. Crowell & Company, 1893, pp. 1–26. [Online] Available http://douglass.speech.nwu.edu/adda_a02.htm (accessed November 1, 1999).

"Why Women Should Vote." *Woman Suffrage: History, Arguments, and Results*. New York: National Woman Suffrage Publishing, 1915, pp. 131–50.

Web Sites

1889 Jane Addams—Hull House. Chicago Public Library. [Online] Available http://cpl.lib.uic.edu/004chicago/timeline/hullhouse.html (accessed November 1, 1999).

International Federation of Settlements and Neighborhood Centers. [Online] Available http://www.ifsderby.demon.co.uk/1index.htm (accessed November 3, 1999).Jane Addams. DISCovering Biography. [Online] Available http://galenet. gale.com (accessed November 1, 1999).

Jane Addams. The Nobel Foundation. [Online] Available http://www.nobel. se/laureates/peace-1931-1-bio.html (accessed November 1, 1999).

Saul Alinsky

Born January 30, 1909
Chicago, Illinois
Died June 12, 1972
Carmel, California

Community organizer

Saul Alinsky united people in low-income neighborhoods to fight discrimination and to demand improvements in housing, education, and city services. He popularized the use of confrontational tactics in the struggle for social change.

Saul Alinsky.
Courtesy of the Library
of Congress.

$\mathcal{S}$aul Alinsky was a self-described "professional radical." (A radical is one who believes that extensive social reform is necessary to cure society's ills.) To those around him, Alinsky was a multifaceted individual: a fighter for the underdog; a chainsmoking, streetwise Jewish intellectual; a confident and confrontational urban populist (advocate for the rights and interests of the common people); and a promoter of participatory democracy (a political system in which every citizen participates in decision-making). In city halls across the United States, where he led noisy protests against the lack of services for poor communities, Alinsky was considered *persona non grata* (Latin term meaning "person who is not welcome.")

Alinsky spent over four decades helping underprivileged Americans fight poverty and injustice and work toward equality in education and working and living conditions. Alinsky began his activist career working with European immigrants in Chicago, Illinois. He eventually made his way across the United States, organizing Mexican Americans in California, African Americans back in his hometown of Chicago, and low-income people in Texas, New York, and Baltimore, Maryland. Alinsky's style of organizing was adopted by activists in the civil rights and antiwar movements.

Childhood in Chicago

Saul David Alinsky was born on January 30, 1909, to Orthodox Russian-Jewish immigrant parents: Benjamin Alinsky, a tailor, and Sarah Tanenbaum Alinsky. At the time of Alinsky's birth the family lived behind Benjamin's tailor shop on Maxwell Street, in a predominantly Jewish, low-income area of Chicago. When Alinsky (an only child) was six years old the family moved to the middle-class, mostly Jewish neighborhood of Douglas Park on the west side of the city.

Alinsky's parents divorced when Alinsky was thirteen years old, after which Alinsky's father moved to Los Angeles, California. Although Alinsky lived with his father for periods of time during high school, contact between the two was eventually lost. Alinsky's relationship with his mother, in contrast, strengthened with time. Sara Tanenbaum was a contentious woman—disagreeable to most people but overly protective toward her son.

Education at the University of Chicago

After graduating from high school, Alinsky enrolled in the University of Chicago. Alinsky majored in archeology and graduated with a bachelor's degree in 1930. He then entered a graduate program in criminology (the study of crime and criminals), with a concentration on social welfare issues.

In graduate school Alinsky conducted research on group organization by studying the pecking order of the Al Capone (1899–1947) gang. (Al Capone was a famous gangster who achieved notoriety in Chicago in the early 1930s as a bootlegger—one who manufactures, sells, or transports alcohol illegall—during the Prohibition era [when the sale of alcohol was illegal].) After gaining the trust of Capone's gangsters, Alinsky was allowed to trail them with notebook in hand. It was during Alinsky's study of Capone's gang that he learned the street lingo and the tough-guy mannerisms that characterized him in later years as an activist.

In 1932 Alinsky left school and went to work with the Chicago Area Project (CAP)—an experimental program aimed at preventing juvenile delinquency. The mission of CAP was to turn troubled youths into community leaders.

Also in 1932 Alinsky married a social worker named Helene Simon. The couple eventually adopted two children. Simon died in 1947 while trying to save a drowning child. Alinsky was wed again in 1952, to a woman named Jean Graham.

Alinsky spent the years 1933 to 1936 working as a criminologist on the parole board at the Illinois State Penitentiary in Joliet. During that time he also engaged in labor organizing for the Congress of Industrial Organizations (CIO) and fund-raising for the International Brigade in Spain (volunteer international army fighting against the authoritarian military dictator Francisco Franco during the Spanish Civil War, 1936–39).

Throughout the 1930s Alinsky wrote several articles for professional criminology journals and gave lectures on social reform. He asserted that the true causes of crime were socioeconomic factors, such as substandard housing, unemployment, lack of health care, and poverty. He criticized state corrections officials for ignoring crime's social roots and for merely focusing on the personal failings of criminals.

The Back of the Yards Neighborhood Council

In 1938 Alinsky returned to Chicago and resumed his involvement with the CAP. He was sent by the CAP to work in Chicago's Back of the Yards neighborhood, a predominantly Irish American slum behind the stockyards. Back of the Yards had gained fame as the setting for Upton Sinclair's 1906 novel *The Jungle*, about the nightmarish working conditions in the meat-packing plants. The neighborhood had been deteriorating for many years; it suffered from crumbling tenements and a lack of city services (such as garbage pick-up and street maintenance). Many of the residents worked under terrible conditions, for low wages, at the meat-packing plants.

Alinsky and his colleague Joseph Meegan, with assistance from labor leaders and local clergy, organized neighborhood residents into a powerful alliance called the Back of the Yards Neighborhood Council (BYNC). BYNC members used tactics such as picketing, rent strikes (refusal to pay rent), and boycotts (refusal to purchase a product or use a service) against slumlords (landlords who make large profits from substandard property), discriminatory businesses, meat-packing companies, and local politicians. The BYNC won a series of dramatic victories, and the lives of local residents improved substantially.

As Alinsky stated in an interview with the *Chicago Daily News* in January 1968, he learned three principles of social action during his BYNC days. The first was: "To hell with charity. The only thing you get is what you're strong enough to get—so you had better organize." The second principle was: "You prove to people they can do something, show them how to have a way of life where they can make their own decisions—and then you get out." Alinsky's third principle was: "It comes down to the basic argument of the *Federalist Papers*. Either you believe in the people, like James Madison and James Monroe, or you don't, like Alexander Hamilton. I do." (The *Federalist Papers* were a series of eighty-five essays in defense of the U.S. Constitution and the newly organized United States government that appeared in newspapers between October 1787 and May 1788.) In 1940 the CAP decided that Alinsky's tactics had become too confrontational for their organization and they removed him from their payroll.

Founds Industrial Areas Foundation

Alinsky moved on from the CAP to found his own organization in 1940—the Industrial Areas Foundation (IAF). The IAF received funding from philanthropist Marshall Field III and an endorsement from Bishop Bernard J. Sheil, Roman Catholic auxiliary bishop of Chicago. The stated purpose of the IAF was to contract with neighborhood organizations to assist in the development of those organizations. Alinsky envisioned the IAF becoming a nationwide network of grassroots, democratic community organizations (such as the BYNC).

In its first decade of existence the IAF trained organizers and assisted with protest actions in scores of communities: in Chicago, the Chelsea district of Manhattan (New York City), neighborhoods near packing houses in South St. Paul (Minnesota) and Kansas City (Kansas), Mexican American barrios (neighborhoods) in California, and elsewhere. Among the young organizers with whom Alinsky worked in California was **César Chávez** (1927–1993; see entry), who later became leader of the United Farm Workers union. Alinsky became something

Alinsky's "for Radicals" books

Saul Alinsky wrote two famous guidebooks for progressive activism: *Reveille for Radicals* in 1946 and *Rules for Radicals* in 1971. *Reveille,* which made the *New York Times* bestseller list, was an appeal to young people to become activists and a practical handbook for community action. In the book, Alinsky defined a "radical" as: "that person to whom the common good is the greatest social value." He explained that in a society dominated by powerful interests, it is imperative that poor people organize themselves into a powerful constituency. If they failed to do that, he argued, they would be left out of the democratic process and their needs would be ignored. He included instructions for transforming neighbor-hood residents into social reformers.

In *Rules for Radicals* Alinsky offered criticism and advice to the "New Left"—young adults active in civil rights and antiwar movements (the Old Left, in contrast, were the activists in the 1920s through the 1950s, many of whom were associated with the Communist Party or the Socialist Party). Alinsky cautioned young activists not to be dogmatic (devoted to certain unbending political ideas), but to be practical and to respect the cultures and traditions of the people they wished to organize. He also recommended that organizers expand their efforts to include the white middle classes, especially in declining urban and suburban neighborhoods.

of an underground hero to working-class people as well as social activists during that era. IAF activities slowed tremendously during the 1950s due to the conservative political climate of the decade.

Begins organizing African American communities

The IAF regained momentum in the late 1950s. At that time Alinsky shifted the foundation's focus toward racial equality and began organizing in African American neighborhoods. Cities that were home to IAF projects in the 1960s included Chicago; Detroit, Michigan; Kansas City, Missouri; Rochester, Syracuse, and Buffalo (the latter three in New York).

The IAF also brought organizers from around the country to its headquarters in Chicago for training workshops.

Alinsky's greatest organizing achievement of the 1960s, for which he gained international recognition, occurred in the predominantly African American Woodlawn section of Chicago (next to the University of Chicago campus). With the backing of local religious leaders, Alinsky's IAF assisted with the formation of The Woodlawn Organization (TWO). Alinsky convinced TWO members to use confrontational tactics in their quest for neighborhood improvement. For example, TWO picketed in the driveway of a landlord's suburban home until that landlord made repairs to his Woodlawn properties. And members of TWO protested the city's lack of sanitation services by dumping their uncollected trash on a city council member's driveway.

"No one in the United States," wrote Charles Silberman about Alinsky in his 1964 book *Crisis in Black and White,* "has proposed a course of action or a philosophy better calculated to rescue Negro or white slum dwellers from their poverty or their degradation." Silberman called Alinsky's efforts in the Woodlawn neighborhood of Chicago "the most important and impressive experiment affecting Negroes anywhere in the United States."

Another of Alinsky's top organizing achievements was FIGHT (Freedom, Independence, God, Honor—Today), a group started in 1965 in a black neighborhood of Rochester, New York. Facing job discrimination, members of FIGHT won concessions from two of the area's largest employers: Xerox and Eastman Kodak. The two corporations agreed to hire more African Americans and to participate in job-training programs. FIGHT also brought city officials to the bargaining table over education and housing concerns.

Alinsky divorced his second wife in 1970 and married his third wife, Irene McInnis, the following year.

IAF outlives Alinsky

Saul Alinsky died of a heart attack on June 12, 1972, in Carmel, California. In a *New York Times* obituary, writer Farnsworth Fowle described how in a typical week Alinsky would "sit down with the Canadian Indians on Monday night, help the Chicanos in the Southwest on Tuesday, be in a blue-collar suburb in Chicago on Wednesday, spend Thursday with white steelworkers in Pittsburgh, move Friday to a black ghetto, and be perfectly happy . . ."

To Alinsky's credit, the organization he founded out-lasted him. Organizers trained by Alinsky have sustained and expanded the IAF in the years since Alinsky's death. The IAF remains a neighborhood empowerment agency headquartered in Chicago, a living testament to the organizational genius of Saul Alinsky.

Sources

Books

Alinsky, Saul. *Reveille for Radicals.* Chicago: University of Chicago Press, 1946.

Alinsky, Saul. *Rules for Radicals.* New York: Random House, 1971.

"Alinsky, Saul David." *Current Biography Yearbook.* Edited by Charles Moritz. New York: H. W. Wilson Company, 1968: 15–18.

Finks, P. David. *The Radical Vision of Saul Alinsky.* New York: Paulist Press, 1984.

Fisher, Robert. "Alinsky, Saul David." *American National Biography.* Vol. 1. Edited by John A. Garraty and Mark C. Carnes. New York: Oxford University Press, 1999.

Horwitt, Sanford D. *Let Them Call Me Rebel: Saul Alinsky, His Life and Legacy.* New York: Alfred A. Knopf, 1989.

Silberman, Charles E. *Crisis in Black and White.* New York: Random House, 1964.

Articles

Fowle, Farnsworth. "Saul Alinsky." (Obituary.) *New York Times.* June 13, 1972.

Wilentz, Sean. Review of *Let Them Call Me Rebel: Saul Alinsky, His Life and Legacy. The New Republic.* December 25, 1989: 30+.

Salvador Allende

Born July 26, 1908
Valparaiso, Chile
Died September 11, 1973
Santiago, Chile

Former president of Chile

Salvador Allende became Chile's first democratically elected Socialist president in November 1970. Allende immediately undertook a series of social reforms aimed at improving the standards of living for Chile's impoverished majority. For his actions Allende was revered by Chile's workers and peasants, yet he was hated by the upper and middle classes, industrialists, and international businesspeople. On September 11, 1973, the Chilean armed forces, with the backing of the United States Central Intelligence Agency, staged a bloody coup. They toppled the Allende government and instated a military dictatorship with General Augusto Pinochet at the helm.

Radical politics a family tradition

Salvador Allende was born on July 26, 1908, in Valparaiso, in central Chile. Allende received an early education in progressive politics from several members of his family. His grandfather had been a founder of the Radical Party (a political party favoring extensive social reform) in the 1860s and his father and his uncles were active in the Radical Party. Allende's mother, Laura Gossens, was a teacher. The young Allende's

"From the very day of our electoral triumph on the fourth of September 1970, we have felt the effects of a large-scale external pressure against us which tried to prevent the inauguration of a government freely elected by the people."

Allende's address to the United Nations in December, 1972.

Salvador Allende.
Reproduced by permission of AP/Wide World Photos.

political education was complemented by lengthy after-school conversations with an anarchist (one who advocates the abolition of government, to achieve full political liberty) shoemaker in his hometown.

After graduating from high school at the age of sixteen, Allende enlisted in the Coraceros Cavalry Regiment, a division of the Chilean armed forces. After completing his tour of duty, Allende enrolled in medical school at the University of Chile.

Years of student activism

During medical school Allende was introduced to the writings of revolutionary socialist thinkers **Karl Marx** (German, 1818–1883; see entry), Vladimir Lenin (Russian, 1870–1924), and Leon Trotsky (Russian, 1879–1940). (Socialism is the belief that the means of production should not be controlled by owners but by the community as a whole.) Allende became active in campus politics. He was elected president of the student medical center and vice-chair of the student federation. He also participated in student protests against the government.

Allende was arrested twice during protests and on one occasion was expelled from the university. It was during his second jailing that Allende received word that his father was dying. Allende was released to visit his father. At his father's funeral Allende vowed to commit his life to the struggle for social change.

Allende was readmitted to school and earned his medical degree in 1932. Because of his reputation as a student radical, however, he had a hard time finding employment in his profession. He worked as a coroner's assistant, a dental school assistant, and a physician at a mental institution before establishing a practice serving poor people in Valparaiso.

Long career in politics

In 1933 Allende helped found the Socialist Party (known by the initials PS, for the Spanish *Partido Socialista*). Allende's first foray into electoral politics came in 1937, when he won the race for representative from Valparaiso and nearby Quillota to the Chilean National Congress. In that role Allende sponsored legislation on matters of public health, social welfare, and women's rights. That same year Allende married Hortensia Bussi, a history teacher. The couple had three daughters.

In the early 1940s Allende served as director of the Ministry of Health, Prevention, and Social Assistance. As such Allende instituted reforms to counter poverty, malnutrition, inadequate health care, substandard housing, and lax industrial safety regulations.

Allende won his first of four elections to the Chilean senate in 1945. His final election to an eight-year term came in 1969. Allende was an extremely popular senator; for nearly ten years he served as either president or vice president of the lawmaking body.

Campaigns for president

Allende ran for president of Chile four times: in 1952, 1958, 1964, and 1970. In his final run, representing a coalition of left-wing parties called Popular Unity, he was successful. Allende did not win an outright majority, but with 36.3 percent he received a greater portion of the vote than either of his two opponents. Allende's ascension to the presidency was ratified by a vote of Congress.

Allende was inaugurated for a six-year term on November 3, 1970. He became the first openly Marxist leader to be democratically elected anywhere in the Western Hemisphere.

Initiates reforms during presidency

When Allende took over as president he began instituting the social reforms he had promised during his campaign—steps that would turn Chile, in his words, into a "republic of the working class." Allende's boldest move was to nationalize (put into government ownership) all copper mines, including the 80 percent owned by U.S. corporations. For this action Allende had the unanimous support of the Chilean legislature. Copper was Chile's most valuable natural resource and greatest export. The Chilean government asserted that the Chilean people—and not foreign business interests—should benefit from its sale.

Allende addressed the problem of landlessness by taking over large estates and converting them into farming cooperatives

Songs of Victor Jara Chronicle the Rise and Fall of Allende's Chile

Accompanying the political reform in Chile was an explosion of cultural expression, including a musical phenomenon known as "new song." No folksinger/songwriter was better known during Allende's presidency than Victor Jara. Jara sang about common Chilean people and their capacity for love, work, and faith. Jara traveled throughout Chile performing for mine workers, peasants, factory workers, students, and children. He was a cultural ambassador of sorts, staging concerts all throughout Latin America.

Victor Jara came to symbolize the empowerment of Chile's impoverished citizens and working classes. For that reason, he was singled out for public torture during the bloody coup in September 1973. Jara was imprisoned in the Chile Stadium along with thousands of other suspected supporters of President Allende during the coup. He sang to the other prisoners to keep their spirits strong. Jara was only silenced when his captors broke the bones in both his hands and killed him with machine guns. In December 1973 the government of General Pinochet issued a directive outlawing the mention of Victor Jara's name in Chile.

Jara composed his final poem, "Estadio Chile" (Chile Stadium), while imprisoned in the stadium. The poem was memorized by several of Jara's fellow prisoners and written down by one who was released. The poem was translated into English by Jara's widow, Joan Jara. It

(farming ventures in which participants work the land and share in the harvests). He undertook ambitious programs to counter hunger, such as providing free milk daily to all schoolchildren.

Rumblings of discontent

Allende's path to socialism may have been peaceful, but it was not smooth. He faced resistance from constituents who felt his reforms went too far and from those who felt his reforms did not go far enough. Members of Chile's middle, upper, and professional classes became increasingly dissatisfied. Some 15,000 wealthy Chileans withdrew their funds and left the country, causing a financial crisis. Others stayed and formed an alliance in opposition to Allende's policies. At the same time, members of the Communist Party, aiming to speed was smuggled out of Chile and released to an international audience. An excerpted version of the poem is presented here.

"Estadio Chile" (Chile Stadium)

There are five thousand of us here
in this little part of the city. . . .
Here alone
are ten thousand hands which plant seeds
and make the factories run.
How much humanity
exposed to hunger, cold, panic, pain
moral pressures, terror and insanity?
Six of us were lost
as if into starry space.
One dead, another beaten as I could never
have believed
a human being could be beaten.

The other four wanted to end their terror—
one jumping into nothingness,
another beating his head against a wall,
but all with the fixed look of death.
What horror the face of fascism
creates! . . . .

How hard it is to sing
When I must sing of horror.
Horror which I am living
Horror which I am dying.
To see myself among so much
and so many moments of infinity
in which silence and screams
are the end of my song.
What I see I have never seen
What I have felt and what I feel
will give birth to the moment

up the land redistribution program, undertook thousands of illegal land seizures in the countryside. The United States and England, both with strong economic interests in Chile, cut off foreign aid and boycotted Chilean exports. These factors and others contributed to an economic crisis and fostered a climate of political discontent.

No parties were more interested in seeing the demise of the Allende government than American economic and political power brokers. After all, the biggest losers in Allende's restructuring were U.S.-based multinational corporations Anaconda and Kennecott. Those two companies owned 80 percent of Chile's copper mines and together controlled four-fifths of Chile's foreign exchange. American corporations held a total of $1 billion in Chilean assets.

Richard M. Nixon, U.S. president at that time, publicly proclaimed neutrality regarding Chile's internal affairs. It later came to light, however, that Nixon had directed the Central Intelligence Agency (CIA; the United States' agency charged with gathering information about foreign governments) to help topple the Allende government. To foster the rebellion, the CIA provided funding to the Chilean military and training in insurrection techniques. The agency also paid to have anti-Allende articles and editorials printed in Chilean newspapers. (The full extent of CIA involvement in the Chilean coup is still not known, since most CIA documents from the era have been sealed. In 1999 the Clinton Administration began a "Chile Declassification Project," which calls for the declassification of documents pertaining the U.S. role in the coup.)

Allende appealed to the world for assistance in a December 1972 address to the United Nations.

> *From the very day of our electoral triumph on the fourth of September 1970 we have felt the effects of a large-scale external pressure against us which tried to prevent the inauguration of a government freely elected by the people, and has attempted to bring it down ever since, an action that has tried to cut us off from the world, to strangle our economy and paralyze trade in our principal export, copper, and to deprive us of access to sources of international financing.*

Military seizes power; Allende dies

On September 11, 1973, the Chilean military, led by army commander Augusto Pinochet, seized power in a bloody coup. The armed forces took over the country's principal ports, then moved in to Santiago where they bombed the Presidential Palace.

In his final address to the nation, on the morning of September 11, 1973, Allende said the following:

> *These are my last words, certain that the sacrifice will not be in vain. I have faith in Chile and its future. Other men will overcome this dark and bitter moment when treason seems to reign. You must never forget that sooner rather than later the grand avenues will be open where free men will march to build a better society. Long live Chile! Long live the people! Long live the workers!*

Allende declined the military's offer of a plane ride out of the country. "As traitorous generals," responded Allende, "you are incapable of knowing what honorable men are like."

Allende chose to remain in the presidential palace, where he and some forty supporters spent five hours warding off continuous air and ground assaults by Pinochet's forces. When the firing and bombing ended, the presidential palace lay in ruins and Allende was dead. By some accounts, Allende committed suicide to avoid being taken prisoner; by other accounts he was murdered.

During and after the coup, several thousand supporters of Allende were rounded up and imprisoned. At least 3,000 Chileans were tortured to death or shot by firing squads (according to some sources, that number was much higher). The exact number of deaths is impossible to know. Bodies were stacked in morgues, left on roadsides, and dumped into the ocean. The ongoing discovery of mass graves continues to drive the number of deaths higher. Among the people killed were some of Chile's most noted writers, professors, physicians, and artists.

Anti-Pinochet demonstration in front of the House of Lords in England during the examination of the validity of Pinochet's arrest by the Lords of Appeal. *Reproduced by permission of the Gamma Liaison Network.*

The arrest of Pinochet

The military junta, with Pinochet at the helm, remained in power until democratic elections were held in 1990. The Pinochet government was repeatedly cited for human rights abuses during its tenure. (Some ten thousand suspected socialists "disappeared" during Pinochet's years in power and were never seen again.) In the fall of 1998, when Pinochet was in England for surgery, Spanish judge Baltasar Garzon took the brazen step of arresting Pinochet on charges of human rights abuses—specifically for the torture of thirty-four Spanish citizens during and after the coup. The eighty-four-year-old Pinochet was found unfit to stand trial in January 2000, thus escaping extradition to Spain. He still faced the possibility of prosecution in his homeland, however.

Following news of Pinochet's arrest, Isabel Allende—novelist and niece of Salvador Allende—stated that the arrest "opened up an incredible window for justice in the world." She added, "A great weight has been lifted in Chile."

In elections held in January 2000, Chilean voters chose Ricardo Lagos to be the first socialist president since Allende. Lagos was a leading dissident during the Pinochet regime.

Pinochet, ailing, returned to his homeland. Despite his age, in August 2000, the Chilean supreme court stripped him of his immunity and ordered him to stand trial.

Sources

Books

"Allende (Gossens), Salvador." *Current Biography Yearbook.* Edited by Charles Moritz. New York: H. W. Wilson Company, 1971, pp. 6–9.

"Salvador Allende." *Historic World Leaders.* Farmington Hills, MI: Gale Research, 1994.

Chavkin, Samuel. *The Murder of Chile.* New York: Everest House Publishers, 1982.

Garza, Hedda. *Salvador Allende.* New York: Chelsea House Publishers, 1989.

Kaufman, Edy. *Crisis in Allende's Chile: New Perspectives.* New York: Praeger, 1988.

Rojas Sandford, Robinson. *The Murder of Allende and the End of the Chilean Way to Socialism.* Translated by Andree Conrad. New York: Harper & Row Publishers, 1975.

Sobel, Lester A., ed. *Chile & Allende.* New York: Facts on File, Inc., 1974.

Articles

"Allende, a Man of the Privileged Class Turned Radical Politician." (Obituary.) *New York Times.* September 12, 1973.

Gallardo, Eduardo. "Quick Trial for Pinochet Unlikely." *Ann Arbor News.* August 8, 2000: A5.

Kornbluh, Peter. "Still Hidden: A Full Record of What the U.S. Did in Chile." *Washington Post.* October 24, 1999: B1+.

"The Pinochet Affair Blackwashing Allende." *The Economist.* January 30, 1999: 34.

Rubin, Sylvia. "'Fortune' Teller: New Novel Marks Isabel Allende's Return to Fiction After a Period of Grieving." *San Francisco Chronicle.* October 12, 1999: B1.

"Try Pinochet in Spain." (Editorial) *St. Louis Post-Dispatch.* October 12, 1999: B14.

Other Sources

Missing. Directed by Constantine Costa-Gavras. Videocassette. 1982.

Jara, Victor. *Manifesto.* Record Album. London, England: Transatlantic Records, 1974.

"Salvador Allende Gossens." *DISCovering Biography.* [Online] Available http://galenet.gale.com (accessed November 2, 1999).

American Friends Service Committee

Founded 1917
Philadelphia, Pennsylvania

Quaker-based international relief and peace-and-justice organization

The American Friends Service Committee was founded during World War I to provide a foreign service alternative for young men being drafted into the U.S. armed services.

The American Friends Service Committee (AFSC) is a humanitarian service organization committed to social justice and peace. The AFSC was founded in 1917 by Quakers (members of the Religious Society of Friends; see box "Who Are the Quakers?") and today is led and staffed by people of various faiths. According to the AFSC Web site, the group's work "is based on the Quaker belief in the worth of every person, and faith in the power of love to overcome violence and injustice."

The AFSC's mission has remained essentially the same throughout the decades: to provide humanitarian relief in war-torn areas around the world, to advocate peaceful solutions to international disputes, and to support struggles for economic independence and civil rights in the United States. The AFSC is headquartered in Philadelphia, Pennsylvania, and has regional offices throughout the United States and in locations where relief projects are underway throughout the world.

The founding of AFSC

In the spring of 1917, just weeks after the United States's entry into World War I (1914–18), Quakers from

AFSC Mission Statement

The mission statement of the American Friends Service Committee reads:

The American Friends Service Committee is a practical expression of the faith of the Religious Society of Friends (Quakers). Committed to the principles of nonviolence and justice, it seeks in its work and witness to draw on the transforming power of love, human and divine.

We recognize that the leadings of the Spirit and the principles of truth found through Friends' experience and practice are not the exclusive possession of any group. Thus, the AFSC draws into its work people of many faiths and backgrounds who share the values that animate its life and who bring to it a rich variety of experiences and spiritual insights.

This AFSC community works to transform conditions and relationships both in the world and in ourselves which threaten to overwhelm what is precious in human beings. We nurture the faith that conflicts can be resolved nonviolently, that enmity can be transformed into friendship, strife into cooperation, poverty into well-being, and injustice into dignity and participation. We believe that ultimately goodness can prevail over evil, and oppression in all its many forms can give way.

around the country held a meeting to discuss the international conflict. Their main concern was helping conscientious objectors (draft-age people who, for religious reasons, oppose all wars) find an alternative way to serve the global community. The result of that meeting was the formation of the American Friends Service Committee. The stated purpose of the new organization was to provide a "service of love in wartime."

The AFSC arranged for Americans who refused military service to conduct relief and reconstruction work in war-torn France. In all, 550 young men and 50 young women participated in the mission (alongside English Quakers), under the sponsorship of the American Red Cross and with the approval of the U.S. government. The AFSC delegation built and repaired homes, cared for refugees, and provided medical care for civilians.

When the war ended, AFSC members remained in Europe to aid with reconstruction. The organization hoped that its efforts would foster reconciliation between nations and avert future wars. In 1920 the AFSC expanded into Germany, where it operated a food relief project through which more than a million German children were fed. AFSC volunteers also assisted with reconstruction in Russia, Serbia, Poland, and Austria.

Relief work abroad

Since its beginnings, the AFSC has conducted relief missions in many parts of the world. The AFSC differs from other religious-based relief organizations in that it does not preach a religious message, nor does it attempt to convert to Christianity the population it is assisting. The AFSC also distinguishes itself by hiring local people to assist with or oversee the design and implementation of projects. The AFSC provides the type of assistance (such as establishing schools and farming cooperatives) that, in the organization's words, "strengthens people's resilience, economic independence, and sense of personal dignity."

The AFSC concentrates most of its relief efforts on war-ravaged regions (particularly places where the U.S. military has been involved); however, it also provides aid to populations struck by natural disaster. In the 1930s the AFSC aided civilians on both sides of the conflict in the Spanish Civil War (the 1936–39 battle between the dictatorial government and opposition forces in Spain). The organization also helped Jewish people leave Germany and Austria and resettle elsewhere in Europe or in the United States to escape the Nazi Party's growing hold on power. (The Nazis—short for the National Socialist German Worker's Party—were an authoritarian and anti-Semitic political and military force headed by Adolf Hitler.)

In the 1940s the AFSC conducted relief operations in Europe, Israel's occupied territories, India, and China. It helped rebuild Korea after the Korean War (1950–53). In the 1960s the AFSC concentrated humanitarian efforts in the war-torn nations of Vietnam and Nigeria. The next decade the group established relief projects in the Middle East and brought aid to drought-plagued African nations.

In the 1980s the AFSC set up schools and cooperatives in postwar Zimbabwe; supplied food, clothing, and medical aid to displaced people in Honduras and Nicaragua; and documented human rights abuses by the U.S.-backed government in El Salvador (for more information, see **Oscar Romero** entry). In the final decade of the twentieth century, the AFSC

Who Are the Quakers?

"Quaker" is a common name for members of the Religious Society of Friends, a religious group founded in 1652 by George Fox in Pendle Hill, England. The term "Quaker" was used to describe the group because its members were said to "tremble at the word of the Lord."

Fox taught that people could directly worship God without clergymen as intermediaries. (At the Friends's religious meetings, elders and other "overseers" preside, and members speak in prayer). As the Religious Society of Friends grew, it drew members away from the Church of England. The English government responded angrily to this trend. It fined and imprisoned Quakers and confiscated their property until the Toleration Act in 1689 brought the government's campaign to a halt.

The Quakers embraced a simple dress code and adopted a thrifty lifestyle. They shunned war, believing that expressions of hatred damage the spirit. As an expression of their faith, they are often involved in welfare work and social reform.

In the late seventeenth century a large number of Quakers immigrated to America and settled on a large land grant given to a Quaker named William Penn in Pennsylvania. In the eighteenth and nineteenth centuries the Quakers played a central role in the movement to abolish (end) slavery in the United States. To this day, the Quakers are known for their refusal to participate in military campaigns and are active in peace and justice work.

provided aid to victims of the 1991 Gulf War in the Middle East (including school supplies for Iraqi children) and delivered food aid to Somalia and Mozambique.

Quakers win Nobel Peace Prize

In 1947 the AFSC, along with its English counterpart the British Friends Service Council, accepted the Nobel Peace Prize on behalf of members of the Religious Society of Friends everywhere. The Quakers were honored for their humanitarian service and their work toward peace and reconciliation.

Gunnar Jahn, chairman of the Nobel Committee, made the following statement upon presenting the Peace Prize to the Quakers on December 10, 1947:

The Quakers have shown us that it is possible to carry into action something which is deeply rooted in the minds of many: sympathy with others; the desire to help others; that significant expression of sympathy between men, without regard to nationality or race; feelings which, when carried into deeds, must provide the foundation of a lasting peace. For this reason they are today worthy of receiving Nobel's Peace Prize.

Peace and justice work in United States

Complementing the AFSC's international relief work are its efforts to promote peace and justice in the United States. The AFSC's domestic agenda includes opposing U.S. military intervention abroad and the stockpiling of weapons, supporting civil rights and liberties, promoting racial reconciliation, assisting economically disadvantaged people, opposing the death penalty, supporting prisoners' rights, and pushing for equal rights for gay men and lesbians.

Since its founding the AFSC has consistently opposed American military involvement in wars and military aid to foreign nations and has counseled young people who object to being drafted into military service. During World War II (1939–45), while prohibited by the U.S. government from sending American conscientious objectors abroad to conduct civilian relief (as they had during World War I), the AFSC established Civilian Public Service camps for young draft refusers. Through that program, conscientious objectors were given work placements in mental hospitals, conservation programs, and training schools. In the 1960s and early 1970s, at the height of the Vietnam War (1954–75), the AFSC counseled draft-age U.S. citizens by the thousands. In 1990 and 1991 the AFSC provided advice and support to conscientious objectors of the Gulf War.

Program of domestic relief

The AFSC's domestic relief program began in the 1920s with food aid to the children of striking coal miners in Appalachia (U.S. region comprising the Appalachian mountains) and material support to striking textile workers in North Carolina. The AFSC's support of coal miners continued in the next decade with the establishment of a homestead program providing land and housing, as well as industrial cooperatives, for unemployed miners.

During World War II the AFSC was one of the few organizations in the United States to oppose Japanese American relocation to detention camps and to provide assistance to the relocated people. (From 1942 to 1945, while the United States fought against Japan in World War II, some 120,000 Americans of Japanese ancestry were imprisoned in camps in the western and central United States.)

In the 1960s the AFSC threw its energies into the civil rights movement. The organization pushed for school desegregation, helping to place seven thousand African American children in schools that were previously all-white. They also participated in campaigns to desegregate public facilities in several cities and helped bring thousands of people to the 1963 March on Washington for jobs and freedom, where nearly a quarter-million Americans heard Martin Luther King, Jr., deliver his famous "I Have a Dream" speech.

In the early 1980s the AFSC worked in support of Native American fishing rights (the rights of Native Americans to fish free from state government interference, in accordance with treaties) and for improved Native American health facilities. In the late 1980s and early 1990s the AFSC attempted to find solutions to homelessness in California, Hawaii, and Massachusetts. As part of that effort, the AFSC worked with an organization of homeless and formerly homeless people in Oakland, California, to build a twenty-six-unit housing complex.

To learn more about the American Friends Service Committee, write to them at 1501 Cherry Street, Philadelphia, Pennsylvania, 19102, or call them at 215–241–7000. Their e-mail address is afscinfo@afsc.org.

Sources

Books

Button, John. *The Radicalism Handbook: A Complete Guide to the Radical Movement in the Twentieth Century.* London, England: Cassell, 1995, p. 355.

Frost, J. William. "American Friends Service Committee." In *Protest, Power and Change: An Encyclopedia of Nonviolent Action from ACT-UP to Women's Suffrage.* Edited by Roger S. Powers and William B. Vogele. New York: Garland Publishing, Inc., 1997.

Jonas, Gerald. *On Doing Good: The Quaker Experiment.* New York: Charles Scribner's Sons, 1971.

Pickett, Clarence E. *For More Than Bread.* Boston: Little, Brown & Co., 1953.

Weisbord, Marvin R. *Some Form of Peace: True Stories of the American Friends Service Committee at Home and Abroad.* New York: Viking Press, 1968.

Web Sites
American Friends Service Committee. [Online] Available http://www.afsc.org/ (accessed April 20, 2000).

American Indian Movement

Founded 1968
Minneapolis, Minnesota

Native American rights organization

The American Indian Movement (AIM) was the best-known and most militant Native American rights organization of the late 1960s and 1970s. (Although AIM still exists today, it commands far less media attention than it did in its heyday.) Comprised of Native American activists from many different tribes, AIM drew attention to the poverty and lack of opportunity plaguing Native American communities in cities and on reservations. AIM undertook militant actions in protest of the injustices inflicted on native people by U.S. government policies—particularly termination (the ending of treaty rights) and relocation (the resettlement of Indians from reservations to cities).

At the time AIM came into being, Native America was in a dismal state. Native American people only lived, on average, forty years, and died from alcoholism, malnutrition, or disease; infants died at a rate twice the national average; unemployment was ten times the national average; at least fifty thousand Indian families lived in dilapidated shacks or castaway cars; the suicide rate for adolescents and teens was the highest in the nation; and alcoholism claimed the lives of Indians under age twenty-four at twenty-eight times the national

"AIM was an indigenous, land-based spiritual movement, a call to the Indian people to return to their sacred traditions and, at the same time, to stand firm against the tide of what they call European influence and dominance."

Rex Weyler in Blood of the Land: The Government and Corporate War against the American Indian Movement.

average. (As recently as 1995 the situation remained much the same: Native Americans still suffered from poverty, unemployment, alcoholism, suicide, and infant mortality at rates far greater than the general population.)

Originates as police watchdog organization

The American Indian Movement (AIM) was founded in 1968 in Minneapolis, Minnesota, by Native American activists seeking to stop the harassment and beatings of Native Americans by white police officers. The group obtained funding from the Urban League (a civil rights organization dedicated to helping minorities in urban areas) of Minneapolis to purchase two-way radios, cameras, and tape recorders, and set up "AIM patrols"—volunteers who would trail the police and document cases of brutality against Indians. AIM leader Vernon Bellecourt said in a July 1973 magazine interview:

> They got evidence of beatings and of ripping people around with handcuffs too tight, ripping their wrists. AIM would show up and have attorneys ready. Often they would beat the police back to the station. They would have a bondsman there, and they'd start filing lawsuits against the police department. . . .

Under the direction of founders Dennis Banks, Russell Means, brothers Clyde and Vernon Bellecourt, Mary Jane Williams, George Mitchell, and others, and with the guidance of elder Pat Ballanger (considered the "Mother of the American Indian Movement"), AIM rapidly established chapters in several cities with large Native American populations. AIM's initial mission of monitoring police behavior in those cities broadened to include a wide range of Native American-rights issues, including respect for tribal self-governance and sovereignty, civil rights and improved housing and employment services for urban Indians, the return of tribal lands to native peoples, and respect for Native American hunting and fishing rights as spelled out in treaties.

The occupation of Mount Rushmore

One of the first high-profile demonstrations organized by AIM was an occupation of the Mount Rushmore National Memorial on September 18, 1970. About fifty Native Americans converged on the national landmark in the Black Hills of South Dakota (featuring enormous sculptures, blasted into the mountainside, of the heads of presidents Abraham Lincoln [1809–1865; president 1861–65], George Washington [1732–1799; president 1789–97], Thomas Jefferson [1743–1826; president 1801–09], and Theodore Roosevelt [1858–1919; president 1901–09]). The group—led by Oglala Sioux activist Russell Means, Lakota Indian and doctoral candidate at University of California-Berkeley Lehman "Lee" Brightman, and Santee Sioux activist **John Trudell** (see entry)—demanded that the United States honor its 1868 Treaty of Fort Laramie with the Sioux nation and return to the Sioux all lands in South Dakota west of the Missouri River, including Mount Rushmore and the rest of the Black Hills.

Upon converging on Mount Rushmore, the group first approached a concessions booth and destroyed a stack of postcards bearing a photograph of Indian bodies piled up following the 1890 Massacre at Wounded Knee. They then took over the stage in the amphitheater usually used by park rangers to speak to tourists. Lee Brightman delivered a speech to a surprised audience about the "true" history of the four presidents whose faces were sculpted into the mountain. He described Washington as an Indian-killer during the French and Indian War (1754–63), Jefferson as the author of a plan to kill all Native Americans in order to "cleanse" North America, Lincoln as the signer of an order to execute thirty-eight Native Americans for the so-called Great Sioux Uprising in Minnesota, and Roosevelt as a thief of Native American land ("he called his booty 'national parks' and 'national forests' to cement the thefts into law," stated Brightman).

The group of Indians climbed the mountain that night and set up camp in an open space behind the sculpture of Roosevelt's head. Supporters from nearby Rapid City brought food, water, and other supplies. The demonstration received national news coverage. Groups of Native Americans remained on Mount Rushmore until that December, when winter storms forced them off. A group of twenty-four Indian activists again scaled Mount Rushmore in protest on June 6, 1971.

AIM's Thanksgiving Day action at Plymouth Rock

Two months after the 1970 Mount Rushmore action,

AIM members conducted a Thanksgiving Day protest near the site of the first pilgrims' landing (at Martha's Vineyard). AIM came at the invitation of Wampanoag Indians still living in the area. According to the Wampanoags, their tribe had been all but wiped out by the very settlers whom the Wampanoag had helped survive for their first two years on this continent. The modern-day Wampanoag people wanted to publicize their understanding of Thanksgiving—that the tradition originated as a feast in celebration of, and giving thanks for, the massacre of the Indians.

Native American activists kicked off their 1970 Thanksgiving Day protest with a march down the highway to a reconstructed pilgrim village called Plymoth Plantation. Beating drums and singing songs, the marchers entered the village dining hall and overturned tables, upsetting the feast. The protesters then headed for the harbor, where a reproduction of the *Mayflower* (the ship on which the original pilgrims came to America) was open to tourists. AIM members boarded the ship, evicted the tourists, took down the American flags, and destroyed displays depicting the pilgrims' version of Thanksgiving. After reaching an agreement with police, who had gathered at the water's edge, the protesters left the ship with guarantees they would not be prosecuted.

During the night, John Trudell and a few compatriots snuck through the fence surrounding Plymouth Rock monument and covered the rock with red paint—symbolizing the blood of the Native Americans on the white men's hands.

Trail of Broken Treaties

AIM took its demands to Washington, D.C., in the fall of 1972 with its famous Trail of Broken Treaties protest. That October, a caravan of cars, trucks, and buses left from the U.S. West Coast, picking up Native Americans at reservations along the way to Washington, D.C. AIM had written to the Bureau of Indian Affairs (BIA) ahead of time, informing the organization of the coming convergence on Washington and presenting its list of twenty demands.

Foremost among the protesters' demands was the repeal of the Indian Appropriations Act of 1871, which had ended the Native Americans' treaty-making status. Other demands included restitution for all treaty violations; the return of 110 million acres of land to native peoples; the revocation of state government authority over Indian affairs; the repeal of termination laws; the reinstatement of government services to unrecognized Indian tribes in the eastern United States; the opportunity to address a joint session of Congress; and the establishment of an Office of Federal Indian Relations and Community Reconstruction in lieu of the Bureau of Indian Affairs.

When the delegation arrived at the BIA, they were turned away at the door. In response, the group took over the building and kicked out BIA employees. The occupation lasted six days. During that time protesters destroyed BIA property and smuggled out files containing evidence of BIA corruption.

The siege came to an end when protesters accepted the government's offer of immunity from prosecution, funds for their transportation home, and consideration of AIM's demands. The government later rejected every point on AIM's list.

The occupation of Wounded Knee

AIM's most famous and confrontational protest occurred over a ten-week period in early 1973, when the group occupied the village of Wounded Knee on the Pine Ridge Reservation of South Dakota. The action took place at the historic site where more than 150 Native Americans had been massacred by U.S. forces in 1890.

The occupation of Wounded Knee began as a quest by Oglala Sioux (or Lakota, the native name for "Sioux") traditionalists (adherents to American Indian cultural practices and religions) to oust their corrupt tribal government. The Indian traditionalists regarded tribal chairman Richard Wilson—as well as his ruthless, BIA-financed police force, the Guardians of the Oglala Nation (commonly referred to as the "GOON squad")—as puppets of the BIA; they believed that Wilson was compromising the interests of the Oglala Sioux people for his personal gain.

On February 28, 1973, several hundred AIM activists and Oglala Sioux traditionalists stormed a church and general store at Wounded Knee. As representatives of national and international media flocked to the scene, the protesters took

Civil rights activists including Rigoberta Menchú (left) support Amnesty International's efforts to gain AIM-activist Leonard Peltier's release.
Reproduced by permission of AP/Wide World Photos.

advantage of the opportunity to publicize the plight of Native Americans in America. According to a *New York Times* dispatch of March 1, 1973, "The embattled Indians relayed demands to Washington that the Senate Foreign Relations Committee hold hearings on treaties made with the Indians, that the Senate start a 'full-scale investigation' of Government treatment of the Indians, and that another inquiry be started into 'all Sioux reservations in South Dakota.'"

Surrounded by superior firepower

Soon after the takeover, the Native Americans occupiers found themselves encircled by heavily armed agents of the FBI and BIA, as well as U.S. marshals and members of tribal and local police forces. The U.S. Army prepared for an invasion by dispatching to the scene seventeen armored personnel carriers, 130,000 rounds of ammunition for M–16 firearms, 41,000 rounds of ammunition for M–1 firearms, 24,000 flares, 12 grenade launchers, 600 cases of tear gas, 100 rounds of M–40 explosives, helicopters, and Phantom jets.

The armed standoff lasted seventy-one days. During that time, AIM leader Russell Means was sent to Washington, D.C., to try to strike a deal with the BIA, but to no avail. Twice during the standoff firefights broke out, resulting in the deaths of two AIM members and one FBI agent.

Negotiations brought the siege to an end on May 8. While the action did not remove Wilson from government, it discredited his administration. In addition, the problems plaguing Native America had been brought to the nation's attention.

AIM suffers retribution by GOON squads

The years following the Wounded Knee siege were

FBI Takes Aim at AIM

AIM was targeted for infiltration and harassment by the Federal Bureau of Investigation (FBI), under its notorious Counterintelligence Program (COINTELPRO). The alleged purpose of COINTELPRO was to combat domestic terrorism. In reality, COINTELPRO was used as a weapon against the anti-Vietnam War and civil rights movements and against militant organizations of people of color.

By the end of the 1970s the FBI's tactics (similar to those used against the **Black Panther Party**; see entry) had greatly diminished AIM's effectiveness. Several AIM members had been killed in firefights with law enforcement officials or had died under mysterious circumstances on reservations. Others associated with AIM—the most famous among them being Leonard Peltier (see entry on **John Trudell**)—had been convicted of serious crimes based on flimsy evidence and imprisoned.

Regarding the FBI's targeting of AIM, activist Dennis Banks stated in a 1977 interview with *Rolling Stone* magazine, "All kinds of strange things have been happening. I suppose [AIM is] 99 percent infiltrated by now."

especially dangerous for AIM members and their supporters on Pine Ridge Reservation. From 1973 to 1975, sixty-nine AIM members living on the reservation were gunned down or died under mysterious circumstances. During the same time period, 350 people associated with AIM were wounded in shootings, stabbings, or beatings—most of them at the hands of the GOON squads.

The Longest Walk

On February 11, 1978, AIM supporters converged on Alcatraz Island (former Native American land and the site of a 1969–71 occupation by Native American activists) for the start of a protest march called The Longest Walk. Participants walked eastward toward Washington, D.C., holding educational workshops along the way on issues facing Native Americans.

The focus of the marchers' discontent was legislation that had been introduced, but not ratified, in the late 1970s that threatened to void the protections guaranteed to Indian tribes by treaties. Participants also publicized the history of Native Americans' forced removal from their homelands and the problems that continued to plague Native American communities. They demanded civil rights, tribal self-rule, and the return of stolen lands.

The Longest Walk ended on July 25 with a demonstration at the Washington Monument, attended by tens of thousands of Native Americans and their supporters. Three days later, twenty-five Native American leaders met with Vice President Walter Mondale and Secretary of the Interior Cecil Andrus to discuss their concerns. One week after that meeting Congress passed a nonbinding resolution calling for religious freedoms for Indians.

Activities in recent years

Although AIM largely faded from public view in the late 1970s, the organization has continued working for improvement of the living conditions of Native Americans. In recent years AIM has focused on the creation and preservation of funding for schools for Native American children called "survival schools," as well as the development of education programs for Native American prisoners. AIM also operates MIGIZI, an Indian news and information service founded in Minneapolis in 1977. In the 1990s AIM was active in the fight against the use of Indian mascots by sports teams such as the Cleveland Indians and Washington Redskins.

Sources

Books

Churchill, Ward, and Jim Vander Wall. *Agents of Repression: The FBI's Secret Wars against the Black Panther Party and the American Indian Movement.* Boston: South End Press, 1988.

Deloria, Vine, Jr. *Behind the Trail of Broken Treaties: An Indian Declaration of Independence.* New York: Dell Publishing Co., 1974.

Grossman, Mark. *The ABC-CLIO Companion to the American Indian Rights Movement.* Santa Barbara, CA: ABC-CLIO, 1996.

Josephy, Alvin M., Jr., ed. *Red Power: The American Indians' Fight for Freedom.* New York: McGraw-Hill Book Company, 1971.

Means, Russell, and Marvin J. Wolf. *Where White Men Fear to Tread: The*

Autobiography of Russell Means. New York: St. Martin's Press, 1995.

Nabakov, Peter, ed. *American Indian Testimony: A Chronicle of Indian-White Relations from Prophecy to the Present, 1492–1992.* New York: Viking, 1991.

Weyler, Rex. *Blood of the Land: The Government and Corporate War against the American Indian Movement.* New York: Everest House, 1982.

Articles
"Armed Indians Seize Wounded Knee, Hold Hostages." *New York Times.* March 1, 1973: 1, 16.

Web Sites
American Indian Movement. [Online] Available http://www.aimovement.org (accessed April 26, 2000).

National Urban Indian Policy Coalition. Report to White House Domestic Council on American Indians (April 10, 1995). [Online] Available http://www.codetalk.fed.us/counrep.html (accessed April 26, 2000).

Amnesty International

Founded May 1961
London, England

International human rights watchdog organization

Police in Guatemala City, Guatemala, beat to death a child living on the streets. Immigration officials in the United States place refugees seeking political asylum in detention, sometimes for years. The Cuban government imprisons a medical doctor for his political opposition activities. Turkish police use electric shock and other forms of torture on criminal suspects. A Moroccan poet is sentenced to fifteen years in prison for the political content of his poems. The Chilean military rounds up and "disappears" thousands of citizens following a coup in 1973. What do these cases have in common? All have been opposed by Amnesty International.

Amnesty International (AI) is an organization dedicated to upholding human rights around the world. According to AI's web site, the group's mandate is to "free all prisoners of conscience. These are people detained anywhere for their beliefs or because of their ethnic origin, sex, color, language, national or social origin, economic status, birth or other status [in 1991 'sexual orientation' was added to the list]—who have not used or advocated violence; ensure fair and prompt trials for political prisoners; abolish the death penalty, torture and other cruel, inhuman or degrading treatment of prisoners; end extrajudicial executions and 'disappearances.'"

AI is respected by national governments and international institutions because of its impartiality (AI does not take sides in political disputes and does not accept funding from any government) and the accuracy of its information. In 1977 AI was awarded the Nobel Peace Prize for its contribution to "securing the ground for freedom, for justice, and thereby also for peace in the world."

The founding of Amnesty International

Amnesty International (AI) was founded in May 1961 by English lawyer Peter Benenson. Benenson had become alarmed by the growing repression against dissenters (those opposed to the established order) in many parts of the world, including Portugal, Spain, East Germany (after World War II [1939–45], Germany was divided into two separate countries, East Germany and West Germany), South Africa, and the Soviet Union. He also took note of the mistreatment of civil rights activists in the United States. After reading about the arrests (and subsequent prison sentences of seven years) of two college students in Portugal who raised their glasses in a toast to freedom in a restaurant, Benenson was prompted to write a letter to his local newspaper, the *London Observer.* His letter, called "The Forgotten Prisoners," was reprinted by newspapers around the world and called for an international campaign to protect human rights and to secure freedom for "prisoners of conscience" (defined as people imprisoned because of peaceful expression of their beliefs, politics, race, religion, color, or national origin).

Within one month of the publication of Benenson's letter, more than a thousand people responded with offers of volunteer assistance and monetary donations. By the end of 1961, those people came together and formed Amnesty International. AI took as its guiding principle the United Nations' Universal Declaration of Human Rights. That 1948 document, drafted after the horrors of Nazi concentration camps in World War II (1939–45) had come to light, advocated the "recognition of the inherent dignity and of the equal and inalienable rights of all members of the human family." (The Nazis—short for the National Socialist German Worker's Party—were an authoritarian and anti-Semitic political and military force headed by Adolf Hitler. Some twelve million people, about half of them Jews, died in Nazi concentration camps during World War II.)

Within one year of AI's founding the organization had established chapters in seven countries, sent delegations to investigate human rights abuses in four countries, and begun fighting—through letter-writing campaigns—for the release of 210 prisoners of conscience. Early on, AI leaders decided to allow activists only to work on cases outside of their own countries. That decision was made both to ensure the impartiality of the process (activists could be influenced by politics within their own country in deciding which allegations of human rights abuse had merit) and to ensure the safety of the activists (many countries with poor human rights records suppress the efforts of human rights advocates).

Organizational structure

Amnesty International has grown dramatically since its founding. In 1999 AI had more than a million members and donors in more than 160 countries. Over 5,300 AI professional and student local groups were operating in more than 90 countries, with national AI networks in 56 countries. The international headquarters of the group was established in London, England, where today some four hundred staff people from fifty countries coordinate the efforts of the various chapters and conduct research to verify the accuracy of information received about human rights abuses.

In addition to pressing for the release of individual prisoners of conscience (in 1998 AI adopted the cause of more than five thousand individuals), AI each year conducts a campaign on human rights abuses in a particular country or a particular human rights issue. For example, in 2000 the focus was on the death penalty (see box titled "Amnesty's Campaign to End the Death Penalty") and in 1999 it was on abuses in the United States (see box "Amnesty Reports Human Rights Abuses in United States"). Each year AI also issues written reports on human rights violations in countries where such violations are widespread (in 1998 AI covered abuses in forty-nine countries).

Amnesty Reports Human Rights Abuses in United States

In October 1998 Amnesty International released a 150-page report about human rights in the United States titled *United States of America—Rights for All.* That publication marked the start of a year-long campaign to expose human rights violations in the United States.

"The report reveals a persistent and widespread pattern of human rights violations in the USA, including police brutality, torture and ill-treatment of prisoners, and a spiraling rate of judicial execution," states Amnesty International on its Web site. "Racism and discrimination contribute to the denial of the fundamental rights of countless men, women and children. . . . [Amnesty International] is raising awareness of the human rights record of a country which often sells itself as a shining light for human rights, and is pressing the USA government to end its reluctance to apply to itself the international human rights standards it so often says it expects of others."

The report includes chapters on police brutality, violations in prisons and jails, the inhumane treatment of foreigners seeking asylum, the death penalty, the exportation of arms to governments that commit torture, and the nation's double standard regarding human rights at home and abroad. It explains that while the United States has strict laws regarding the protection of civil rights and human rights, those laws are regularly broken by police officers, prison guards, and immigration officials.

"Ultimately, when a society fails to care what happens to some of its members, believes that certain human beings have forfeited their human rights because of their actions, or fails to hold officials to account for their misdeeds," wrote the report's authors in the introduction, "then it creates the conditions in which human rights violations can thrive."

Urgent Action network

One of AI's most critical functions is operating an Urgent Action (UA) network. This network provides assistance for prisoners or others facing imminent human rights abuses—such as torture or execution. When AI hears about such cases, staffers at the London headquarters send urgent action alerts to chapters around the world. From there, the alerts are distributed to approximately eighty thousand UA volunteers in eighty-five countries. The volunteers send messages to officials

On the 50th Anniversary of the Peoples Republic of China
中华人民共和国建立的五十周年
FREE all Prisoners of Conscience
请把所有的良心犯释放
Jiang Zemin
江泽民
Amnesty International

President Jiang Zemin
FREE
Hada
Mongolian bookseller
CHINA
Prisoner of Conscience

President Jiang Zemin
FREE
Liu Jingsheng
Trade Unionist
CHINA
Prisoner of Conscience

President Jiang Zemin
FREE
DIGNITY
Zhang Lin
Labour activist
CHINA
Prisoner of Conscience

Amnesty International demonstration outside Buckingham Palace against human rights violations in China. The demonstration was prompted by Chinese president Jiang Zemin's visit to London, England, in 1999.

Reproduced by permission of Corbis Corporation (Bellevue).

in the designated country demanding respect for the rights of the individuals in danger. The messages are sent by e-mail, telegram, or fax, in order to reach their destinations as quickly as possible.

In 1998 the UA network was activated 425 times, on behalf of individuals in ninety-four countries. There were three thousand to five thousand appeals sent in each case. The appeals have been shown to work (to alleviate or stop the human rights abuses) in about one-third of all cases.

Amnesty targets torture

One of AI's primary objectives is to end torture. Torture is defined in the United Nation's Declaration of Human Rights as "cruel, inhuman or degrading treatment or punishment." Examples of torture include severe beatings, electric shocks administered to the genitals or tongue, burning with cigarettes, sleep deprivation, hanging by arms or legs, and

Activists, Rebels, and Reformers

Amnesty's Campaign to End the Death Penalty

Amnesty International kicked off the new millennium with a campaign for a moratorium (suspension) on executions. AI opposes the death penalty on many grounds, such as the lack of proof that the death penalty works as a deterrent against violent crime, the influence of racism in the imposition of the death penalty, and the fact that there is no "undoing" the death penalty if the executed person should later be proven innocent. The organization points out that more than half the world's countries do not use capital punishment and that there are other ways to effectively protect society from violent criminals.

AI is working to collect millions of signatures on the following petition:

An Appeal for a Moratorium of the Death Penalty by the Year 2000.

We, the undersigned, are convinced that the death penalty:

- *Is the denial of the right to life, which is universally recognized*

- *Is the final, cruel, inhuman and degrading punishment*

- *Is inadequate to stop violence; it actually legitimizes an irreversible act of violence by the state and society which cuts off human life*

- *Dehumanizes our world by putting vengeance and reprisal first; it eliminates clemency, forgiveness and rehabilitation by the justice system. . . .*

For these reasons we appeal to all governments of the world to observe a moratorium of the death penalty by the year 2000.

For more information, visit the Amnesty International Web site against the Death Penalty at http://www.web.amnesty. org/rmp/dplibrary.nsf/Moratorium?openview.

---

feigning a prisoner's execution (for example, firing a blank round at a prisoner's head). AI estimates that two-thirds of the world's inhabitants live in countries where torture is used. AI has documented that torture, in the form of police brutality, even occurs in industrialized nations such as the United States, France, and Great Britain.

"Torture is a fundamental violation of human rights," states an AI pamphlet, " . . . an offense to human dignity and prohibited under national and international law." AI pressures governments to outlaw torture and prosecute those who commit torture and pleads for the rights of individuals who are subjected to torture.

Sources

Books

Amnesty International USA. *United States of America: Rights for All.* London, England: Amnesty International Publications, 1998.

Bronson, Marsha. *Amnesty International.* New York: New Discovery Books, 1993.

Button, John. *The Radicalism Handbook: A Complete Guide to the Radical Movement in the Twentieth Century.* London, England: Cassell, 1995, p. 357.

DeAngelis, James J., ed. *Public Interest Profiles 1998–1999.* Washington, D.C.: Congressional Quarterly, Inc., 1998.

Drinan, Robert F. "Nongovernmental Organizations Effectively Combat Human Rights Abuses." In *Human Rights: Opposing Viewpoints.* Edited by Bruno Leone, et al. San Diego: Opposing Viewpoints Series, 1998.

Larsen, Egon. *A Flame in Barbed Wire: The Story of Amnesty International.* New York: W. W. Norton & Company, 1979.

Staunton, Marie, and Sally Fenn, eds. *The Amnesty International Handbook.* Claremont, CA: Hunter House, 1991.

Web Sites

Amnesty International. [Online] Available http://www.web.amnesty.org (accessed March 26, 2000).

Ella Jo Baker

Born December 13, 1903
Norfolk, Virginia
Died December 13, 1986
New York, New York

Organizer for NAACP and SCLC; advisor to SNCC

E lla Baker was a brilliant behind-the-scenes organizer, considered by many to be the "godmother" of the civil rights movement. She championed the ideal of grassroots empowerment and member-controlled leadership in civil rights organizations. She was a living example of her own philosophy that the best leaders are those who empower others to lead.

In an activist career spanning fifty years, Baker established numerous chapters of the National Association for the Advancement of Colored People (NAACP) and sparked the formation of both the Southern Christian Leadership Conference (SCLC) and the **Student Nonviolent Coordinating Committee** (SNCC; see entry). And by taking an active role in political affairs at a time when women were expected to remain on the sidelines of society, Baker served as a role model for a generation of young women.

Youth and education

Ella Baker was born in 1903 in Norfolk, Virginia, the second of three children. Her father was a waiter, and her

"The best country in the world, you hear them say. I guess it may be. I haven't lived anywhere else. But it's not good enough as far as I'm concerned."

Ella Baker in Moving the Mountain *by Ellen Cantarow.*

Ella Baker.
Courtesy of the Library of Congress.

mother was a schoolteacher who was active in the church and community affairs. When she was eight years old, Baker moved with her family to Littleton, North Carolina. For the next seven years Baker lived on land that her grandparents had once worked as slaves but later purchased after they were set free. Baker attended high school in Raleigh, North Carolina, and then attended the predominantly black Shaw University. She graduated from Shaw in 1927, at the top of her class.

Later that year, Baker moved to Harlem, in New York City. She spent the next two years working in a factory and waitressing. In 1929 Baker accepted a position on the editorial staff of the *American West Indian News*.

Early activist positions

Baker began her career as a social activist in 1932, during the Great Depression (the worst economic crisis ever to hit the United States; it began in 1929 and continued through the late 1930s). Her first activist position was as director of the Young Negroes Cooperative League, a branch of the Works Progress Administration (WPA; one of the many social programs initiated by President Franklin Delano Roosevelt [1882–1945; president 1933–45] to provide jobs and pull the nation out of the Depression). In that capacity, Baker helped people form buying cooperatives so they could purchase food and other goods in large quantities and thus save money.

In the mid-1930s Baker was also active in a women's rights organization called the Women's Day Workers and Industrial League. She wrote a book in 1935 titled *Crisis,* which exposed the miserable working conditions of domestic servants.

Works with the NAACP

Baker joined the NAACP in 1938 and in 1940 was named national director of branches (also known as field secretary). Her main responsibility was to recruit members throughout the American South. She also promoted job training programs for African American workers. Baker resigned from the national NAACP in 1946, due to differences with the organization's cumbersome bureaucracy and top-down leadership style. She felt that the organization would be stronger if the grassroots constituency were empowered to make its own decisions, rather than taking directions from national leaders.

In the late 1940s and early 1950s Baker worked as a freelance consultant to numerous civil rights groups, two of which were the National Urban League (an African American community service organization active primarily in cities) and In Friendship (a New York-based organization that raised funds for civil rights activists in the South). Baker quickly earned a reputation as an effective organizer.

In 1954 Baker became president of the New York City NAACP. In the mid-1950s she organized parents to fight for racial integration of public schools. (Although the 1954 *Brown v. Board of Education* Supreme Court ruling outlawed segregation in public schools, it took several more years before most school districts allowed integration to proceed.)

Formation of the Southern Christian Leadership Conference

In December 1956 Baker approached **Martin Luther King, Jr.**, (1929–1968; see entry) with the idea of forming an organization of African American ministers to coordinate civil rights activities in the South. King, at the time, was president of the Montgomery Improvement Association—the organization that had coordinated the successful, 382-day-long, Montgomery, Alabama, bus boycott. Baker, who had been one of the boycott's strongest supporters in the North, was impressed by the ability of King and other ministers to rally large numbers of participants. Baker felt that the momentum of the boycott should be preserved.

After some debate, King agreed with Baker's idea of forming a permanent organization. The Southern Christian Leadership Conference (SCLC) was founded in January 1957 by sixty-five African American ministers from eleven southern states. The group set up headquarters in Atlanta, Georgia, and selected King as president. The ministers hired Baker as acting executive director and office manager.

Baker's role in the group's success has been greatly overlooked in most history books. As an experienced activist, Baker navigated the group through the murky political waters of the period. During her two-and-a-half years with the SCLC,

Fannie Lou Hamer: Another Heroine in the Movement

Another brave African American woman at the fore of the struggle for civil rights was Fannie Lou Hamer. Hamer was born in 1917 in Montgomery County, Mississippi, the youngest of twenty children of sharecropper parents. When Hamer was two years old, her family moved to a plantation in the flat Delta lands of Sunflower County—the county she was to call home for the rest of her life.

Hamer's family worked hard in the fields, with little to show for it. At one point the family saved enough money to buy some livestock, with the dream of starting their own farm. The white landowners quickly extinguished that dream by poisoning the animals.

Hamer toiled in the fields until the age of forty-four. A turning point in her life came in August 1962, when she attended a voter-registration meeting organized by the **Student Nonviolent Coordinating Committee** (SNCC; see entry). Hamer then attempted to register to vote, only to lose her home and her job as retribution. Hamer remained undeterred from her civil rights activities, even after she was severely beaten in jail and received numerous death threats.

Hamer became one of the civil rights movement's most forceful organizers and most eloquent spokespersons. In her

---

Baker was the group's senior strategist, producer and distributor of literature, and public relations director. She also coordinated the group's voter registration program, called Crusade for Citizenship.

"The kind of role that I tried to play (at the SCLC)," stated Baker in the 1980 book about women activists titled *Moving the Mountain,* "was to pick up pieces or put together pieces out of which I hoped organization might come. My theory is, strong people don't need strong leaders."

The birth of SNCC

In April 1960 Ella Baker organized a conference at Shaw University, in Raleigh, North Carolina, for members of the student sit-in movement. (Sit-ins were a form of civil rights protest in which African American students, sometimes joined by

Fannie Lou Hamer. *Reproduced by permission of AP/Wide World Photos.*

famous speech before the Democratic Party National Convention in August 1964, as a representative of the Mississippi Freedom Democratic Party, Hamer asked: "Is this America, the land of the free and the home of the brave where we have to sleep with our telephones off the hooks because our lives be threatened daily because we want to live as decent human beings?" That speech served as a wake-up call to the nation regarding the dire situation of African Americans in Mississippi.

Until her death in 1977, Hamer devoted all her energies to fighting for the political and economic rights of poor people and people of color.

white students, would request service at segregated lunch counters, department stores, or other places of business; they refused to leave when denied service.) Baker felt that students, with their boundless energy and optimism, had a great potential to bring about social change. She urged them to form an organization through which they could coordinate their actions.

The three largest civil rights organizations—SCLC, NAACP, and CORE (Congress on Racial Equality)—sent representatives to the conference to try to convince the students to form a wing of their respective organizations. Baker, however, steered the students away from associating with any of the established civil rights organizations. She advised them to form an independent organization that would reflect, and respond to, the needs and experiences of the students. The new student organization, she argued, should be energetic and militant, and not cautious and conservative like the established groups.

"We ended up with about three hundred people [at the conference]," stated Baker in an interview in the late-1970s. "The Southern Christian Leadership Conference was interested in having the students become an arm of the SCLC. They were most confident that this would be their baby, because I was their functionary and I had called the meeting. The SCLC leadership made decisions about who would speak to whom to influence the students to become part of the SCLC. Well, I disagreed. I wasn't one to say yes, just because it came from the Reverend King."

Baker also sought to foster the students' natural tendency toward participatory democracy or, as Baker called it, "group-centeredness." The established civil rights organizations were all led by strong directors who made the decisions and handed down instructions to the membership. Baker, in her years with the NAACP and the SCLC, had become disillusioned with the top-down leadership style. The sign of a healthy organization, according to Baker, was "the development of people who are interested not in being leaders as much as in developing leadership among other people."

The result of the Shaw University conference was the birth of the **Student Nonviolent Coordinating Committee** (see entry), better known by its initials SNCC (pronounced "snick"). Baker stayed with SNCC through the early 1960s as an informal counselor. She gave strategy advice, helped resolve conflicts between members, and introduced the students to older activists in the South she had met while working for the NAACP. SNCC quickly rose to the fore of the civil rights movement. Its activists were recognized as hardworking, fearless, and committed warriors in the fight for racial equality.

Helps found the Mississippi Freedom Democratic Party

In 1964 Baker assisted Mississippi civil rights activists in founding a new political party, the Mississippi Freedom Democratic Party (MFDP). The MFDP was organized as an alternative to the regular Democratic Party, which excluded African Americans. Baker gave the keynote address at the MFDP convention in Jackson, Mississippi, and set up the MFDP's Washington, D.C., office.

On August 6, 1964, delegates from the MFDP (including legendary Mississippi civil rights organizer Fannie Lou Hamer; see box) headed for Atlantic City, New Jersey, where they challenged the regular Democratic Party for representation of the people of Mississippi at the national Democratic presidential convention. Baker was instrumental in drumming up support in the capital for the MFDP's challenge. Although the MFDP was unable to unseat the regular Democratic Party, they forced a change in rules to favor integrated state party delegations at future conventions and dramatized the plight of African Americans from Mississippi before a national television audience.

Active in her later years

Baker remained active in the fight for civil rights and human rights even as a senior citizen. She worked for liberation in Africa and fought racism in America. She was also active in women's rights groups and labor organizations, was a national board member of the Puerto Rican Solidarity Committee, and served as an advisor to students opposing the Vietnam War (1954–75). Baker was in constant demand as a speaker at conferences and demonstrations throughout the United States.

"Maybe there will be a new revolution," Baker said in an interview in the late-1970s. "I don't think there's going to be one anytime soon, to be honest—I mean among blacks or whites in this country. The best country in the world, you hear them say. I guess it may be, I haven't lived anywhere else. But it's not good enough as far as I'm concerned."

Baker died of natural causes in 1986, on her eighty-third birthday, in Harlem in New York City. A few years before Baker's death, a documentary about her life titled *Fundi: The Story of Ella Baker* aired on public television. "Fundi" is a Swahili (a language spoke in some parts of Africa) word for "one who hands down a craft from one generation to the next."

Sources

Books

Cantarow, Ellen. *Moving the Mountain: Women Working for Social Change.* Old Westbury, NY: The Feminist Press, 1980.

Carson, Clayborne. *In Struggle: SNCC and the Black Awakening of the 1960s.* Cambridge: Harvard University Press, 1981.

Clinton, Catherine. "Ella Baker." *The Reader's Companion to American History.* Boston: Houghton Mifflin Co., 1991: 71–72.

Crawford, Vicki L., Jacqueline Anne Rouse, and Barbara Woods, eds. *Women in the Civil Rights Movement: Trailblazers and Torchbearers, 1941–1965.* Brooklyn, NY: Carlson Publishing, Inc., 1990.

Dallard, Shyrlee. *Ella Baker: A Leader Behind the Scenes.* Englewood Cliffs, NJ: Silver Burdett Press, Inc., 1990.

Engelbert, Phillis. *American Civil Rights.* 4 Vols. Farmington Hills, MI: U•X•L, 1999.

Giddings, Paula. *When and Where I Enter: The Impact of Black Women on Race and Sex in America.* New York: Bantam Books, 1984.

Grant, Joanne. *Ella Baker: Freedom Bound.* New York: John Wiley & Sons, Inc., 1998.

Levy, Peter B. *The Civil Rights Movement.* Westwood, CT: Greenwood Press, 1998.

Mills, Kay. *This Little Light of Mine: The Life of Fannie Lou Hamer.* New York: Dutton, 1993.

Robinson, Jo Ann Gibson. *The Montgomery Bus Boycott and the Women Who Started It.* Knoxville: University of Tennessee Press, 1987.

Robnett, Belinda. *How Long? How Long? African-American Women in the Struggle for Civil Rights.* New York: Oxford University Press, 1997.

Salmond, John A. *My Mind Set on Freedom: A History of the Civil Rights Movement, 1954–1968.* Chicago: Ivan R. Dee, 1997.

Articles

Cantarow, Ellen, and Susan Gushee O'Malley. "NAACP, SCLC, SNCC: Ella Baker Got Them Moving." *Ms.* June 1980: 56+.

"Rites Held in New York for Rights Activist Ella Baker." (Obituary) *Jet.* January 19, 1987: 18.

Wiley, Jean. "On the Front Lines; Four Women Activists Whose Work Touched Millions of Lives: Fannie Lou Hamer, Ella Baker, Amy Jacques Garvey, and Septima Clark." *Essence.* February 1990: 45+.

Other Sources

Fundi: The Story of Ella Baker. [videocassette] Grant, Joanne. New York: Icarus Films, 1986.

Judi Bari

Born November 7, 1949
Baltimore, Maryland
Died March 2, 1997
Willits, California

Environmentalist, labor organizer,
and peace activist

Judi Bari devoted her final ten years to the campaign to save California's ancient redwood trees. As a member of the militant environmental organization Earth First! she advocated a nonviolent, direct-action approach to protecting old-growth forests. Bari made it clear that timber company executives—not workers in the forests—were the parties responsible for the plunder of the forests. She attempted to build alliances with loggers, recognizing that their livelihood was also affected by the irresponsible actions of the timber company executives.

Bari's effectiveness as an organizer and dedication to her cause gained her the respect of environmentalists and the ire of logging interests and law enforcement agencies. In 1990 Bari was permanently crippled by a bomb that exploded under her seat as she drove her car. The Federal Bureau of Investigation (FBI) accused Bari of transporting the bomb for her own purposes—a charge Bari vigorously refuted. Bari, in turn, charged the FBI with complicity in the bombing and sued the agency, as well as the Oakland police, in federal court. In 1997, as the case lingered in the justice system, Bari died of cancer. The question of who bombed Bari remains unanswered.

"I was attracted to Earth First! because they were the only ones willing to put their bodies in front of the bulldozers and the chainsaws to save the trees."

Judi Bari in a 1992 interview by Ms. *magazine*

Judi Bari.
Reproduced by permission of AP/Wide World Photos.

Upbringing in Baltimore

Bari was born on November 7, 1949, in Baltimore, Maryland, to Arthur and Ruth Bari. She was one of three daughters in a middle-class family. As a child Bari learned to play the violin. (She later played her instrument to boost the morale of participants at political demonstrations.)

Bari attended the University of Maryland in the late 1960s and early 1970s, during the height of U.S. involvement in the Vietnam War (1954–75). She devoted so much of her time as a student to the antiwar movement that she later said she had majored in "anti-Vietnam War rioting." Bari left school during her fifth year.

Works as labor organizer

In the early 1970s Bari worked as a clerk in a supermarket. She became a union shop steward and entered the world of labor organizing. Also during that time the five-foot-tall Bari began learning karate for self-defense. She eventually attained the rank of black belt.

Bari next took a job at a bulk mail center of the U.S. Postal Service. To get the position she had to prove that she was able to lift a seventy-pound sack of mail—something that few women applicants had achieved. Bari continued her organizing activities at the plant, including publishing a newsletter highlighting worker concerns. In an effort to secure better working conditions, Bari led the workers on a successful wildcat strike (a labor strike that has not been sanctioned by union officials).

Moves to California

In 1979 Bari moved to Santa Rosa, California, with her boyfriend Mike Sweeny. Shortly thereafter the two were wed. They had two daughters and later divorced. In the early and mid-1980s Bari was active in the Pledge of Resistance—a group working to end U.S. support for repressive governments in Central America. She also participated in abortion-rights demonstrations.

In the mid-eighties Bari and her family moved to northern Mendocino County, California, where Bari trained to be a carpenter. One of her first projects was to construct her own cabin in the hills above the old logging town of Willits, California.

Bari's foray into environmental activism came while she was building a beautiful country home for a corporate executive. She asked about the origin of the exquisite lumber being used as siding and was horrified to learn that it came from ancient redwood trees. (Redwoods are the world's tallest, oldest trees. They take four hundred to five hundred years to reach maturity and some have been around for two thousand years. Due to destructive forest practices, only 3 percent of America's ancient redwood forests remain.) "A light bulb went on," stated Bari in a 1990 interview. "We are cutting down old-growth forests to make yuppie houses. I became obsessed with the forests." (Yuppie is an acronym for "young, upwardly-mobile professional".)

Becomes environmental defender

In 1988 Bari joined the environmental organization Earth First! (see box), which was devoted to halting logging in old-growth redwood forests. She set up an office for the organization in the Mendocino Environmental Center in Ukiah, California, and became the group's contact person in Mendocino County.

The first logging protest Bari helped organize was near Cahto peak, in northern Mendocino County's Coast Range mountains. Bari and other activists blocked loggers' access to the forest. In part due to their efforts, the several-thousand-acre forest in question was designated the Cahto Wilderness Area and was made off limits to logging. Bari rapidly became recognized as the movement's most eloquent speaker.

Fights for rights of timber workers

Bari's background as a labor organizer made her sensitive to issues facing timber workers. She was adamant that environmentalists treat the workers as allies in the fight against unsustainable (unable to maintain over the long run) logging practices. Bari stressed that the timber corporations' policy of overcutting was not only harming the environment but was also leaving so few trees as to necessitate the phasing-out of loggers' jobs.

Earth First!

Earth First! is a militant environmental organization that uses direct-action tactics to defend natural areas. The group endorses the philosophy of "deep ecology," which underscores the interdependence of all plant and animal species and calls for the restoration of vast areas of wilderness.

Earth First! members are known for blocking logging roads with their bodies, chaining themselves to road-building equipment, and sitting in trees to prevent the trees from being cut down. The organization has also embraced "ecotage," the damaging of bulldozers, chainsaws, and other equipment used to clear forests. (Bari convinced the group to give up "tree spiking"—the practice of driving long metal spikes into trees, which not only damaged chainsaws but inadvertently caused injuries to some workers.)

"I was attracted to Earth First! because they were the only ones willing to put their bodies in front of the bulldozers and the chainsaws to save the trees," stated Bari in a 1992 interview in *Ms.* magazine. "They were also funny, irreverent, and they played music. But it was the philosophy of Earth First! that ultimately won me over. This philosophy, known as biocentrism or deep ecology, states that the earth is not just here for human consumption. All species have a right to exist for their own sake, and humans must learn to live in balance with the needs of nature, instead of trying to mold nature to fit the wants of humans."

In 1989, when workers at a Georgia-Pacific sawmill in Fort Bragg, California, were accidentally doused with oil containing PCBs (polychlorinated biphenyls—organic chemicals known to cause cancer in humans), Bari stood up for them. She helped organize the workers into a local chapter of the Industrial Workers of the World (IWW; radical labor union that seeks to unite all of the world's workers) and supported their efforts to hold Georgia-Pacific accountable in U.S. Labor Court.

Bari's predictions of overcutting of the forest began to come true in April 1990, when Lousiana-Pacific (LP) closed one sawmill. As a result, 195 workers were laid off. Bari accompanied a group of LP workers to a meeting of the Mendocino County Board of Supervisors. There Bari explained that LP was cutting trees at too rapid a rate and proposed that the county

Earth First! demonstration at the Lincoln Memorial in Washington, D.C. *Reproduced by permission of Corbis Corporation (Bellevue).*

take over LP's three hundred thousand acres of wooded land and operate them in the public interest.

"In Mendocino County since 1990," stated Bari in a 1996 interview in the *San Francisco Examiner*, "Louisiana Pacific laid off more than two-thirds of its workers and closed five of its seven mills. What we've been saying is true: It's corporations versus the rural community. We've never said no to logging. We just want sustainable logging."

Organizes Redwood Summer and Forests Forever

In the spring of 1990 Bari and fellow Earth First! organizer Darryl Cherney began executing a plan, called Redwood

Summer, to bring thousands of college students from around the state to northern California, where they could participate in a summer-long campaign to protect the old-growth redwood forests. The program was named for, and attempted to invoke the spirit of, the 1964 Freedom Summer program (see entry on **Student Nonviolent Coordinating Committee**) in which students went to Mississippi to conduct civil rights organizing.

At the same time, Bari championed Earth First's "Forests Forever Initiative" (Proposition 130) on California's fall 1990 ballot. The proposition, if passed, would have slowed the pace of logging in the state's forests, or in Bari's words, prevented "liquidation logging." Timber companies joined forces in an underhanded but ultimately successful campaign to defeat the measure. The timber companies' efforts included labeling Earth First! members as "eco-terrorists" and issuing bogus press releases on Earth First! stationery advocating violence.

During the Forests Forever campaign Bari, Cherney, and other advocates of the proposition began receiving death threats. Bari was threatened over the phone and in letters. One threat against her, delivered to the door of the Mendocino Environmental Center, contained a newspaper photo of Bari with the telescopic sight of a gun drawn over her face. Attached was a yellow ribbon—the symbol of the movement in opposition to the ballot initiative. When Bari reported that ominous message and other threats to the police, she was told, "When you turn up dead, then we'll investigate."

Seriously injured in car bombing

On May 24, 1990, Bari was nearly killed when a motion-triggered bomb exploded. The bomb, planted under Bari's car seat, went off as she drove with Darryl Cherney to a college campus to recruit volunteers for Redwood Summer. The explosion cracked Bari's pelvis in ten places and broke her spine. It left her with a paralyzed foot and in constant pain. Cherney suffered cuts on his face and ruptured eardrums, which caused temporary deafness.

The FBI and Oakland, California, police accused Bari and Cherney of placing the bomb in the car themselves. They arrested the pair for transporting explosives (for alleged use against logging companies) and held them on $100 thousand bond—even as Bari was hospitalized in an intensive care unit. Bari and Cherney vehemently denied any involvement in the bombing and two months later were cleared. Since police could not come up with any evidence of the pair's culpability, charges were never brought against them. The police and the FBI, however, refused to investigate the case further. They claimed that Bari and Cherney remained the only suspects.

In 1991 Bari and Cherney filed a civil rights lawsuit in federal court against the FBI and Oakland police for falsely arresting them, trying to discredit them as "terrorists," fabricating evidence against them, and failing to seek out the real bombers. Also named in the suit were several individual law enforcement officers, including Richard Held, the FBI Special Agent in charge of the San Francisco, California, office at the time of the bombing. Held's involvement is noteworthy because he headed the FBI's efforts to discredit and destroy the **Black Panther Party** (see entry) and the **American Indian Movement** (AIM) (see entry) under the agency's Counterintelligence Program (COINTELPRO) of the 1960s and 1970s. (In COINTELPRO, FBI agents gathered information on and attempted to destroy the anti-Vietnam War movement, the civil rights movement, and militant organizations of people of color.)

"This case is not about me or Darryl or Earth First!" Bari wrote in the *Earth First! Journal* shortly before her death. "It is about the right of all activists to work for social change without fearing repression by their own government's secret police."

Dies of cancer

Even after the bombing, Bari continued her fight to protect the forests. In 1992 she helped coordinate a two-month-long campaign—involving road blockades, the chaining of activists to logging equipment, and sit-ins in trees—to stop logging on land along Mendocino County's coastal Albion River. And in 1995 Bari was the first of hundreds of people to be arrested at a rally protesting the logging of the world's last unprotected groves of ancient redwoods, in the Headwaters Forest in Humboldt County.

In 1997 Bari was diagnosed with breast cancer. She refused to be hospitalized or undergo chemotherapy, choosing instead to live out her final months in the comfort of her home. The cancer spread to her liver and on March 2, 1997, she died. Bari was forty-seven years old.

"It's important that we pay tribute to our heroes, and Judi Bari is definitely one of those," stated former congressman Dan Hamburg during a February 2, 1997, call-in show dedicated to Bari on Philo, California's, KZYX public radio station. Speaking directly to Bari, he said, " . . . You're truly a revolutionary. You see . . . a different kind of world; a world where connections are made between the global economy and poverty and environmental deterioration. . . . [You will] always be remembered as a great person in the movement for the world we all want to see come about."

Sources

Books

Button, John. *The Radicalism Handbook: A Complete Guide to the Radical Movement in the Twentieth Century.* London, England: Cassell, 1995, pp. 375–76.

Harris, David. *The Last Stand: The War between Wall Street and Main Street over California's Ancient Redwoods.* New York: Times Books, 1995.

Helvarg, David. *The War Against the Greens.* San Francisco: Sierra Club Books, 1994.

Scarce, Rik. *Eco-Warriors: Understanding the Radical Environmental Movement.* Chicago: The Noble Press, Inc., 1990.

Articles

Bishop, Katherine. "Militant Environmentalists Planning Summer Protests to Save Redwoods." *New York Times.* June 19, 1990: A18.

Martin, Glen. "2,000 Protest Plan to Log Old-Growth Redwoods." *San Francisco Chronicle.* September 16, 1995: A1+.

Martin, Glen. "Earth's Still First." *San Francisco Chronicle.* June 11, 1995: 6+.

McKinley, Jesse. "Judi Bari, 47, Leader of Earth First Protest on Redwoods in 1990." (Obituary.) *New York Times.* March 4, 1997.

Reed, Christopher. "Force of the Green Fuse." (Obituary.) *The Guardian* (London). March 5, 1997: 15.

Vollers, Maryanne. "Who Bombed Judi Bari?" *Harper's Bazaar.* August 1996: 100+.

Web Sites

Judi Bari Web Site of the Redwood Summer Justice Project. [Online] Available http://www.monitor.net/~bari/ (accessed March 27, 2000).

Daniel J. Berrigan
Born May 9, 1921
Virginia, Minnesota

Philip F. Berrigan
Born October 5, 1923
Two Harbors, Minnesota

Jesuit priests and peace activists

Daniel and Philip Berrigan were both ordained as Jesuit priests in the 1950s. They became adherents of a secular (worldly) religious philosophy that promotes the improvement of the human condition, or the creation of a "heaven" here on Earth. Daniel and Philip Berrigan came into the public eye in 1967 and 1968, when they were arrested and served time in prison for dramatic protests against the Vietnam War (1954–75). The brothers' involvement in peace and justice issues has been unfailing, from their civil rights and anti-Vietnam war activism of the 1960s and 1970s to their antinuclear weapons activism of the 1980s and 1990s.

"Our apologies, good friends, for the fracture of good order. The burning of paper [draft records], instead of children . . . when will you say no to this war? . . . This war stops here."

From an open letter by Daniel Berrigen.

Sons of a union activist

Daniel and Philip Berrigan were born in northern Minnesota: Daniel on May 9, 1921, in the town of Virginia; and Philip on October 5, 1923, in the town of Two Harbors. They were the youngest of six sons, and two of three siblings to enter the priesthood. The Berrigans' father, Thomas Berrigan, was a union activist and a socialist (one who believes that the

Philip (left) and Daniel Berrigan (right).
Reproduced by permission of UPI/Corbis-Bettmann.

means of production should not be controlled by owners, but by the community as a whole).

Because of his activism, Thomas was fired from his job on the railroad when his children were young. The family moved to a farm near Syracuse, New York, where Thomas co-founded the Syracuse local of the Electrical Workers Union and the Syracuse chapter of the Catholic Interracial Council. The children attended a Catholic school and worked on the family farm. The Berrigans, despite being poor themselves, provided food and shelter to needy people during the Great Depression (the worst economic crisis ever to hit the United States, from 1929 through the late 1930s).

Entry into priesthood

In 1939 Daniel enrolled in Woodstock College. Upon graduation he entered the Jesuit school of theology at Weston, Massachusetts, and began a twelve-year course of intense spiritual and intellectual training. (The Jesuits, or Society of Jesus, are a religious order in the Roman Catholic Church.) He was ordained as a Jesuit priest in 1952.

Philip played semiprofessional baseball and worked as a janitor on trains after high school. He then spent one semester St. Michael's College in Toronto, Canada, before being drafted into the U.S. armed forces in 1943. Philip was sent to the southern United States for boot camp training. There he was deeply disturbed by the racial discrimination he witnessed against African Americans in the military. After his tour of duty in Europe in World War II (1939–45), Philip enrolled in Holy Cross Seminary. He graduated with a bachelor's degree and then entered the seminary of the Society of St. Joseph (Josephite Order of Jesuits) in Newburgh, New York. Philip's brother Jerome had already entered the order, which had been established in England in 1866 and came to the United States in 1871 to assist newly liberated slaves. Philip was ordained a Josephite priest in 1955.

Political awakenings

Both Daniel and Philip were concerned about world affairs when they entered the priesthood; their experiences as members of the clergy served to intensify those concerns. In

1953 Daniel was sent to France by his religious order, where he spent a year with priests who had been active in the Nazi resistance (the group that opposed Adolf Hitler's Nazi forces during World War II). From those priests he learned about civil disobedience (nonviolent action in which participants refuse to obey certain laws, with the purpose of challenging the fairness of those laws).

Upon his return from Europe, Daniel spent three years teaching French and theology (the study of religion) at a Jesuit preparatory school in Brooklyn, New York. In 1957 he began a six-year stint teaching at LeMoyne College in Syracuse. During that period he was active in civil rights and antipoverty activities. In the early 1960s Daniel founded the Catholic Peace Fellowship.

Philip, after his ordination, was assigned to be a counselor at the all-African American St. Augustine High School in New Orleans, Louisiana. In response to the racial discrimination and poverty he witnessed around him, Philip became very involved with the civil rights movement. He took part in Freedom Rides (bus rides throughout the American South by integrated groups of people, to test the enforcement of a pair of Supreme Court rulings disallowing segregated seating on interstate buses and trains) and worked with the **Student Nonviolent Coordinating Committee** (SNCC; a student civil rights organization that engaged in voter registration activities and nonviolent protests in the 1960s; see entry).

Opposition to the Vietnam War

In 1963 Philip was transferred to the St. Joseph seminary in New York City. The following year he was moved to Epiphany College in Newburgh, New York, where he served as an instructor in English. By that time the war in Vietnam was raging. Young men were being returned to the United States in body bags by the thousands, and the nightly news was filled with horrifying images of burning fields and dead Vietnamese villagers. Philip became an outspoken critic of U.S. foreign policy, describing the U.S. aggression in Vietnam as the mirror image of the government's policies of racial and economic injustice at home.

In one particularly fiery speech Philip asked whether it would be "possible for us to be vicious, brutal, immoral, and

Writings of the Berrigan Brothers

Both Daniel and Philip Berrigan are authors of impressive lists of essays, books, poems, plays, and speeches. In 1966 the Berrigan brothers coauthored *They Call Us Dead Men: Reflections on Life and Conscience.*

Daniel's earliest publications, which reflected his growing radicalism, included: *Time without Number* (1957); *The Bride: Essays in the Church* (1959); *The Bow in the Clouds: Man's Covenant with God* (1961); and *The World for Wedding Ring, Poems* (1962). Four of Daniel's books were written while he was in prison and include his reflections on civil disobedience and its consequences. One of Daniel's prison writings was a one-act play, titled *The Trial of the Catonsville Nine*, about the court proceedings following his arrest for burning draft records. That play was awarded the Frederick G. Melcher Book Award from the Unitarian Universalist Association. His 1971 work, *The Dark Night of Resistance*, won the National Book Award. In 1987 he published *To Dwell in Peace: An Autobiography*. In all, Daniel has written eighteen books of poetry and more than thirty books of prose.

Philip Berrigan's first book, published in 1965, was a collection of essays called *No More Strangers*. He has written scores of journal articles plus eight books since that time. Two of his books—*Prison Journals of a Priest Revolutionary* and *Widen the Prison Gates: Writing from Jails, April 1970–December 1972*—were written while he was imprisoned. Philip's autobiography, *Fighting the Lamb's War: Skirmishes with the American Empire*, was published in 1996.

violent at home and be fair, judicious, beneficent, and idealistic abroad." Shortly thereafter, the Jesuits reprimanded Philip and transferred him to a parish in inner-city Baltimore.

Daniel returned to the United States in 1964, following a year's sabbatical in Europe, to join the antiwar movement. He was assigned to a New York City parish where he edited the journal *Jesuit Missions*. Daniel founded the organization Clergy Concerned About Vietnam in the mid 1960s and organized sit-ins (protests in which participants refuse to leave the premises of a military center, lawmaker's office, or other place associated with the war effort), pickets, and teach-ins (educational seminars by antiwar activists at colleges and universities) against the war.

In 1966 Daniel became the director of religious work at Cornell University in Ithaca, New York. The following year he led a group of antiwar activists to demonstrate in front of the Pentagon (headquarters of the U.S. Department of Defense), where he and several others were arrested. In early 1968 Daniel traveled to North Vietnam to negotiate the release of American prisoners of war.

Dramatic protests against the Vietnam War

The Berrigan brothers participated in sensational protests against the Vietnam War in 1967 and 1968 that resulted in their arrests. Philip, on October 27, 1967, entered a Selective Service (draft board) office in Baltimore, Maryland, with three other activists. The group poured duck blood on draft records—a poignant symbol of the human blood being spilled in Vietnam. The group then quietly prayed and waited to be arrested.

On May 17, 1968, when Philip was free on bond awaiting trial, the Berrigans plus seven others entered a Selective Service office in Catonsville, Maryland (near Baltimore). To the surprise of clerks on duty, they removed draft records from file cabinets and placed them in trash cans. They took the trash cans to the parking lot and burned the files with homemade napalm (a chemical used by the U.S. military to burn vegetation and villages in Vietnam).

In an open letter by Daniel explaining this action, he wrote: "Our apologies, good friends, for the fracture of good order. The burning of paper, instead of children . . . when will you say no to this war? . . . This war stops here." Daniel later wrote an award-winning play about the action, which was performed widely around the country, titled *The Trial of the Catonsville Nine*.

Philip was sentenced to six years in prison for the Baltimore action and three-and-a-half years for the Catonsville action, to be served concurrently (at the same time). Daniel received a prison sentence of three-and-a-half years for his part in the Catonsville action.

Berrigans go underground to avoid prison

Both brothers went underground (into hiding) rather than enter prison. Philip remained a fugitive for twelve days before being captured at a church by agents of the Federal Bureau of Investigation (FBI). Daniel remained underground for four months before his capture. During that time, while being pursued by the FBI, Daniel even made public appearances. Daniel's capture was aided by information contained in private correspondence between Philip and a friend, photocopied by an FBI informant.

Philip served three years of his sentence and Daniel served less than two years. Both brothers passed their time in prison writing poetry and essays. In 1971 the FBI charged the brothers with conspiring to blow up government targets in Washington, D.C., and kidnap government officials. The charges were dismissed in 1972.

Philip marries and leaves priesthood

Philip secretly married a nun named Elizabeth McAlister in 1969. When the church learned of Philip's marriage, Philip was excommunicated (cut off from membership). Philip and Elizabeth (who eventually had three children) established Jonah House in Baltimore—a community of nonviolent resisters and social justice activists.

Philip continued his campaign against militarism in 1976, when he and twenty-one others threw red paint (to symbolize blood) on military aircraft at an exhibit in East Hartford, Connecticut. The protesters were arrested. Once it was determined that there had been no property damage, however, the charges were dropped.

Commitment to peace remains strong

The Berrigan brothers continued to involve themselves in issues of peace and justice. Daniel remained a Jesuit priest in New York City and an instructor at Woodstock College. He was active in the movement against U.S. intervention in Central America in the 1980s, visiting both El Salvador and Nicaragua. He continues to work with peace groups and counsels people with AIDS (acquired immunodeficiency syndrome—a disease that weakens the victim's immune system, leaving the body unequipped to fight off a wide range of illnesses).

Philip cofounded the Plowshares witnesses—a group of activists who engage in civil disobedience to protest the nuclear arms buildup. "Plowshares" is taken from the biblical passage: "beat your swords into plowshares." One of Philip's earliest Plowshares actions occurred in 1980, when he and seven others entered the General Electric factory in King of Prussia, Pennsylvania, and took hammers to nuclear missile nose cones. For his part in Plowshares actions between 1980 and the mid-1990s, Philip served a total of seventy-three months in jail. In 1998, at the age of seventy-five, Philip was sentenced to two years in prison for damaging a Navy guided-missile destroyer.

Sources

Books

"Berrigan Brothers." *Religious Leaders of America,* 2nd ed. Farmington Hills, MI: The Gale Group, 1999.

"Berrigan, Daniel." *Encyclopedia of World Biography.* Farmington Hills, MI: The Gale Group, 1998.

Berrigan, Daniel. *America is Hard to Find.* New York: Doubleday & Company, Inc., 1972.

Berrigan, Daniel. *To Dwell in Peace: An Autobiography.* San Francisco: Harper & Row Publishers, 1987.

Berrigan, Philip. *Prison Journals of a Priest Revolutionary.* New York: Holt, Rinehart and Winston, 1967.

Berrigan, Philip. *Widen the Prison Gates: Writing from Jails April 1970–December 1972.* New York: Simon & Schuster, 1973.

"Daniel and Philip Berrigan." *Contemporary Heroes and Heroines.* Vol. 1. Edited by Ray B. Brown. Detroit: Gale Research, 1990.

Articles

Anderson, George M. "Daniel Berrigan at 75: An Interview." *America.* April 27, 1996: 14+.

Berrigan, Daniel. "Daniel Berrigan on Contemporary Developments in American Spirituality." *Tikkun.* September–October 1998: 47+.

Berrigan, Philip. "Fighting for Disarmament." *Tikkun.* May–June 1998: 23+.

"Is Anyone Listening to the Prophets Anymore?" *U.S. Catholic.* August 1996: 6+. Interview with Daniel Berrigan.

Lockwood, Lee. "Still Radical After All These Years." *Mother Jones.* September–October 1993: 14.

"Sentenced, Philip Berrigan." *Time.* April 6, 1992: 64.

Black Panther Party

Founded 1966
Oakland, California
Disbanded around 1980

African American self-defense and community improvement organization

"Standing on our constitutional and democratic human rights, we made Malcolm X's philosophical polemics, 'the ballot or the bullet' and 'by any means necessary,' come alive."

Black Panther Party cofounder Bobby Seale in Seize the Time.

Black Panther Party founders: Bobby Seale and Huey Newton.
Reproduced by permission of AP/Wide World Photos.

The Black Panther Party (BPP) used arms and traditional organizing techniques to protect and uplift embattled African American communities. In an effort to curb police brutality against African Americans, BPP squads—carrying guns, cameras, and law books—followed police throughout the streets at night. BPP chapters throughout the United States also offered free community services such as breakfast programs, health clinics, schools, clothing distribution, and shoe repair shops.

Because of their antigovernment militancy, the Panthers were labeled by the Federal Bureau of Investigation (FBI) as a "threat to the security of the United States." FBI agents and local police forces used a variety of methods to destroy the Panthers. By the end of the 1960s, twenty-eight Panther leaders had been killed by police and hundreds of others had been jailed.

Founding of the Black Panther Party

The Black Panther Party (BPP) was established in Oakland, California, in October 1966, as a revolutionary nationalist (devoted to the interests of one's own nation, ethnic group, or cultural group) organization committed to stopping police brutality and improving living conditions in African American communities. (Originally called the Black Panther Party for Self-Defense, the group dropped the "for Self-Defense" in 1967). The BPP's founders were two African American men who had met at Oakland's Merritt College: twenty-four-year-old Huey Newton (1942–1989) and twenty-nine-year-old Bobby Seale (1937–). The pair also worked together at the North Oakland Neighborhood Anti-Poverty Center, where they frequently encountered African Americans who had been brutalized by the police.

The name "Black Panther" was taken from a political party organized by **Student Nonviolent Coordinating Committee** (SNCC; see entry) members in 1966 in Lowndes County, Alabama. As Newton and Seale wrote about their party's adopted symbol, "It is not in the panther's nature to attack anyone first, but when he is attacked and backed into a corner, he will respond viciously and wipe out the aggressor."

Seale and Newton drafted a ten-point program for the BPP, calling for jobs, decent housing, quality education, an end to police brutality, and political freedoms (see box). The authors referred to black America as a "colony" within the United States and demanded that African Americans be allowed to decide their national destiny in a plebiscite (election) sponsored by the United Nations.

The BPP gradually swelled in number. Panthers could be recognized by their berets and black leather jackets, and by the rifles they carried at their public appearances (in 1966 it was legal to carry weapons in full view in California). BPP leaders instilled discipline by putting members through military-style drills. The Panthers also started a weekly newspaper, called *The Black Panther*, that covered incidents of police brutality and editorialized against racism.

Demonstration at California state house makes headlines

The Black Panthers attracted national media coverage on May 2, 1967, when they demonstrated against proposed gun-control legislation at the California state house in Sacramento. The legislation being debated, which later became law,

RETALIATION TO CRIME: REVOLUTIONARY VIOLENCE
RÉPONSE AU CRIME: LA VIOLENCE RÉVOLUTIONNAIRE
RESPUESTA AL ASESINATO: VIOLENCIA REVOLUCIONARIA

"Black Power."
Reproduced by permission of AP/Wide World Photos.

proposed banning the carrying of loaded weapons in public. The bill had been written in direct response to the Panthers' self-defense activities.

A group of twenty-four armed Panthers marched in military formation to the capital building and attempted to enter the visitors gallery. Their presence caused a great commotion. Prevented by police from reaching the visitors gallery, they stopped in the lobby, and Bobby Seale read a prepared statement (the Panthers' first communication to the American public).

> *The Black Panther Party for Self-Defense calls upon the American people in general and the black people in particular to take careful note of the racist California Legislature which is now considering legislation aimed at keeping the black people disarmed and powerless at the very same time that racist police agencies throughout the country are intensifying the terror, brutality, murder, and repression of black people. The Black Panther Party for Self-Defense believes that the time has come for black people to arm themselves against this terror before it is too late. . . .*

The Panthers involved in the protest were arrested; many were charged under obscure laws regulating fishing and hunting. Huey Newton, identified as the mastermind of the protest (although he was not present), was also arrested and sentenced to four months in jail.

Undergoes philosophical shift

By late 1969 the BPP had established chapters in forty-four cities (among them Los Angeles, California; Kansas City, Missouri; New York, New York; Chicago, Illinois; and Denver, Colorado) and a handful of foreign countries, with a total membership of several thousand people (the number ranges from five thousand to thirty thousand, depending on the source consulted). Around that time, the Panthers underwent a subtle shift in philosophy. While the group had always pushed for economic empowerment of poor people as well as black nationalism (the creation of institutions that would make African Americans politically, economically, and socially self-sufficient), around 1969 the group's primary emphasis shifted from race to class.

The BPP at the turn of the decade came to embrace socialism (social and economic organization based on the control of the means of production by the community as a whole, rather than by wealthy individuals or corporations). And while remaining an all-black organization, the Panthers became more willing to form alliances with radical organizations of whites and people of other races.

Sponsors community initiatives

In the late 1960s the BPP also placed a growing emphasis on community service programs. The Panthers sponsored a popular free breakfast program for children in forty-four cities. In addition, they maintained health clinics, alternative schools, and other services in several inner-city areas. Numerous chapters helped homeless people find housing and unemployed people find jobs, and distributed food to needy people.

Targeted by COINTELPRO

The Black Panther Party was selected for infiltration and destruction under the FBI's notorious Counter-Intelligence Program (COINTELPRO). COINTELPRO operatives were ordered by FBI Director J. Edgar Hoover (1895–1972) in August 1967, "to expose, disrupt, misdirect, discredit, or otherwise neutralize the activities of black nationalist, hate-type organizations and groupings, their leadership, spokesmen, membership and supporters, and to counter their propensity for violence and disorder." In 1968 FBI agents were told to intensify their campaign against the Black Panthers and, in the words of Hoover, "to exploit all avenues of creating dissension within the BPP" and to "submit imaginative proposals designed to cripple the BPP."

The FBI used a number of methods in its successful quest to bring down the Panthers. For example, undercover FBI agents posing as black militants joined the BPP and encouraged the members to plot illegal acts. The agents then delivered information about planned activities to the police. When the acts were carried out, police officers would appear and arrest the offenders.

Undercover FBI agents also sowed seeds of distrust within the BPP. For instance, agents who joined the BPP would

The Black Panthers' Ten-Point Program, 1966 and 1972

Newton and Seale first authored the Panthers' ten-point program—a list of demands for the white power structure—in October 1966. Philosophical changes in the group (primarily the shift in emphasis from racial solidarity to economic class solidarity) provoked the rewriting of the ten-point program in March 1972. Below are both versions of the ten-point program.

1966 ten-point program

1. We want freedom. We want power to determine the destiny of our Black Community.

2. We want full employment for our people.

3. We want an end to robbery by the white man of our Black Community.

4. We want decent housing, fit for shelter of human beings.

5. We want education for our people that exposes the true nature of this decadent American society. We want education that teaches us our true history and our role in the present-day society.

6. We want all black men to be exempt from military service.

7. We want an immediate end to **police brutality** and **murder** of black people.

8. We want freedom for all black men held in federal, state, county and city prisons and jails.

9. We want all black people when brought to trial to be tried in a court by a jury of their peer group or people from their black communities, as defined by the Constitution of the United States.

10. We want land, bread, housing, education, clothing, justice and peace. And as our major political objective, a United Nations-supervised plebiscite to be held throughout the black colony in which

issue false threats against a particular activist or faction in the name of another activist or faction. In one case, bogus correspondence initiated by FBI agents led to a shootout between the Panthers and a rival organization in which two Panthers died.

Police take aim at BPP

Enraged by Panther slogans such as "off the pigs" (meaning "kill the cops"), the police sought any opportunity to retaliate against Black Panthers. A number of Panther leaders were lured into shoot-outs with police and arrested. The only black colonial subjects will be allowed to participate, for the purpose of determining the will of black people as to their national destiny.

1972 ten-point program

1. We want freedom. We want power to determine the destiny of our Black and oppressed communities.

2. We want full employment for our people.

3. We want an end to robbery by the capitalist of our Black and oppressed communities.

4. We want decent housing, fit for the shelter of human beings.

5. We want education for our people that exposes the true nature of this decadent American society. We want education that teaches us our true history and our role in the present-day society.

6. We want completely free health care for all Black and oppressed people.

7. We want an immediate end to police brutality and murder of Black people, other people of color, all oppressed people inside the United States.

8. We want an immediate end to all wars of aggression. [Note: this applies to international and domestic conflicts against oppressed people.]

9. We want freedom for all Black and poor oppressed people now held in U.S. federal, state, county, city and military prisons and jails. We want trials by a jury of peers for all persons charged with so-called crimes under the laws of this country.

10. We want land, bread, housing, education, clothing, justice, peace and people's community control of modern technology.

first high-profile case was that of Huey Newton. In 1967 Newton engaged in a gun battle in which a police officer was killed. Newton, who was seriously wounded, was charged with voluntary manslaughter. He was convicted and imprisoned but was freed when his conviction was overturned in 1970.

From 1968 to 1970 police conducted a number of raids on BPP chapters. Seventeen-year-old Bobby Hutton, the Panther's treasurer, was killed during a police raid on an Oakland house in which several Panthers were living. And twenty-year-old Fred Hampton, head of the Illinois Black Panthers, as well as Panther activist Mark Clark, were killed in their beds during

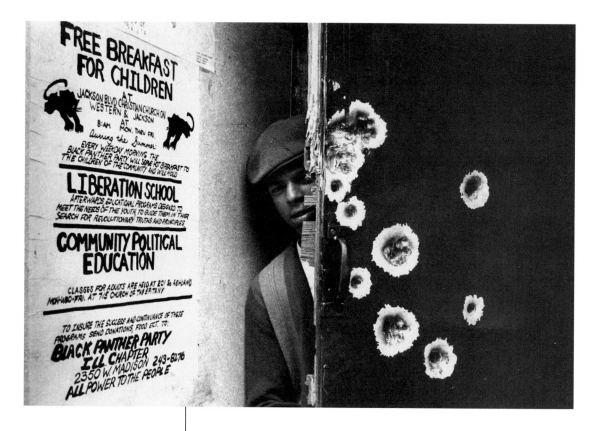

By the early 1970s many Black Panther chapters closed. Because of constant harassment by the police and FBI, they were no longer able to run their community service programs, such as the Free Breakfast for Children program.
Reproduced by permission of Corbis Corporation (Bellevue).

a predawn raid on their apartment by Chicago Police. By the end of the 1960s police officers had killed twenty-eight Black Panthers.

The Los Angeles BPP lost its leader, Geronimo Pratt, in 1971. Pratt was convicted of murder based on the testimony of a key witness, later identified as an FBI informant, and sentenced to life in prison. (In 1985 the witness recanted his testimony, but Pratt's conviction stood. Pratt was finally released in 1997 after a court found that prosecutors had suppressed key evidence in his original trial.) And in New York City twenty-one BPP activists were charged with conspiracy to bomb department stores, police stations, and railroad tracks. With bond set at $100 thousand each, twelve of the activists were forced to spend the months before and during their trial in jail. All of the New York twenty-one were eventually acquitted. By the end of 1971 more than three hundred Black Panthers were behind bars or had been forced into exile.

The demise of the Panthers

Occupied with protecting themselves from police raids and FBI infiltration, the Panthers were left with little time or resources for community organizing. By the early 1970s, with many of its leaders either dead or in prison, the BPP foundered. Many chapters closed up shop.

Elaine Brown, the Panther's first female leader (and Huey Newton's longtime companion), breathed new life into the Oakland chapter in 1974. She resurrected the free breakfast program and organized an award-winning educational center for poor children. Under Brown's leadership, the Panthers remained active in Oakland through the late 1970s.

Sources

Books

Churchill, Ward, and Jim Vander Wall. *Agents of Repression: The FBI's Secret Wars against the Black Panther Party and the American Indian Movement.* Boston: South End Press, 1988.

Dello Buono, Richard A. "Black Panther Party." In *The African American Encyclopedia.* Vol. 1. Edited by Michael W. Williams. New York: Marshall Cavendish, 1993, pp. 171–74.

Haskins, Jim. *Power to the People: The Rise and Fall of the Black Panther Party.* New York: Simon & Schuster Books for Young Readers, 1997.

Seale, Bobby. *Seize the Time: The Story of the Black Panther Party and Huey P. Newton.* Baltimore: Black Classic Press, 1991. First published by Random House in 1970.

Web Sites

"History of the Black Panther Party." [Online] Available http://www.stanford.edu/group/blackpanthers/history.shtml (accessed March 29, 2000).

Unita Blackwell

Born March 18, 1933
Lula, Mississippi

Mayor and civil rights activist

"You organize around the moment. You do it moment by moment, day by day, and it turns into a great work. But you don't see it at the time."

Unita Blackwell, interview by Essence *magazine, 1998.*

Unita Blackwell.
Reproduced by permission of AP/Wide World Photos.

U nita Blackwell was inspired to join the civil rights movement in the early 1960s by student activists. She registered voters, helped found the Mississippi Freedom Democratic Party, and worked to improve housing conditions in low-income African American communities throughout the American South. In retaliation, Blackwell was arrested and jailed more than seventy times and had a cross burned on her lawn by the Ku Klux Klan (a group that advocates white supremacy).

In 1976 Blackwell was elected mayor of Mayersville, Mississippi, the town where she had lived since 1960. She then led an initiative to incorporate Mayersville as a legally recognized municipality, in order to bring basic services to the town's residents. With only an eighth grade education, Blackwell returned to school and earned a master's degree in regional planning. In 1989 Blackwell was elected to head the National Conference of Black Mayors. In 1992 she was awarded a prestigious MacArthur Foundation "genius" grant.

A childhood of poverty

Blackwell was born in Lula, Mississippi, on March 18, 1933, during the Great Depression (the worst economic crisis in the history of the United States, from 1929 through the late 1930s). This period, while difficult for people of all racial groups, was especially hard on African Americans. While unemployment for the nation overall reached 25 percent, unemployment for African Americans exceeded 50 percent.

Blackwell's parents were farm workers. They followed the harvests throughout Arkansas, Mississippi, and Tennessee, attempting to make ends meet. After finishing only the eighth grade, Blackwell joined her family working in the fields and factories, picking cotton and peeling tomatoes through her young adulthood. Blackwell lived a migratory lifestyle until 1960, when she settled in a three-room shack in the town of Mayersville, with her husband and young child.

Introduction to civil rights movement

Blackwell, like other African Americans in the pre-civil rights South, had essentially no political rights. And Blackwell's home state of Mississippi, nicknamed the "closed society," was undeniably the most segregated (separated by race) state in the country.

While African Americans made up 45 percent of the population in Mississippi, in 1960 only 5 percent of all African Americans in the state were registered to vote. African Americans were prevented from registering to vote by literacy tests (selectively administered to African American applicants, these tests required would-be voters to read and/or interpret a section of the state Constitution to the satisfaction of the registrar), economic intimidation (such as threats of job loss), and outright violence. Mississippi had the South's highest number of lynchings, beatings, and unexplained disappearances of African American residents. (Lynching is the extra-legal execution of a person [usually an African American] accused of a crime or a violation of social standards, often by hanging, by a group of three or more people.)

In 1964 Blackwell was drawn into the civil rights movement—the organized effort of thousands of individuals to secure the right to vote, freedom from discrimination in

Robert Moses: SNCC's Coordinator in Mississippi

The coordinator of the **Student Nonviolent Coordinating Committee's** (SNCC; see entry) efforts in Mississippi from 1961 through 1964 was Robert Parris Moses (1935–). Moses was a soft-spoken mathematics teacher who had grown up in New York City's Harlem River Projects. He held a bachelor of arts degree from Hamilton College (in upstate New York) and a master's degree in philosophy from Harvard University in Cambridge, Massachusetts.

Moses became interested in the civil rights movement in 1960. He moved to Atlanta, Georgia, and began working with SNCC. In 1961 Moses was one of a handful of SNCC members to conduct voter registration efforts in Mississippi—at that time, the most segregated state in the nation. Moses endured beatings and jailings and witnessed the killings of his co-workers, to help black Mississippians secure the right to vote.

In the 1964 Moses helped recruit and train approximately one thousand volunteers—many of them white students from northern colleges—for "Freedom Summer" in Mississippi. In late June 1964 Freedom Summer volunteers conducted door-to-door voter-registration drives and established community centers, "freedom schools," health clinics, legal clinics, and community feeding sites called "freedom kitchens."

Moses also helped lay the foundation for a new political party, the Mississippi Freedom Democratic Party (MFDP). The MFDP was set up as an

employment, and other civil rights for African Americans. Her first contact with civil rights workers came one Sunday morning when a member of the **Student Nonviolent Coordinating Committee** (SNCC, pronounced "snick," an organization of student civil-rights activists formed in 1960; see entry), came to the church where Blackwell was teaching Sunday school to talk about voter registration. Blackwell was one of eight people to volunteer to go to the courthouse the next day to try to register. Blackwell was turned away at the courthouse and soon thereafter lost her job chopping cotton. In the months to come, the Ku Klux Klan burned a cross on Blackwell's front lawn in an attempt to intimidate her. In *Women in the Civil Rights Movement: Trailblazers and Torchbearers, 1941–1965*, Blackwell is quoted:

Robert Moses. *Courtesy of the Library of Congress.*

traveled to the national Democratic Party convention in Atlantic City, New Jersey, where they challenged the regular Democratic Party for recognition as the true representatives of the people of Mississippi.

After resigning from SNCC in 1965 Moses was an active opponent of the Vietnam War (1954–75). In 1968 he moved to Tanzania, in Africa, where he taught high school and raised a family. Moses moved back to the United States in 1977. Four years later he was awarded the MacArthur Foundation's "genius" grant (the same grant awarded to Blackwell in 1992). Moses returned to Mississippi in 1992 to found the Delta Algebra Project— a mathematics instruction program for disadvantaged youths.

alternative to the regular Democratic Party, which excluded African Americans. Moses and the rest of the MFDP delegation

I got angry that another human being could tell me that I didn't have a right to register and was going to deny me this right. I got mad and I was determined that I wasn't gonna take no more. . . .

[SNCC] told me that I had natural instincts in organizing techniques. I organized whole counties. . . . You organize around what the needs of the people are. People needed decent housing to stay in; they needed food . . . You tell them that if they register to vote, then we'll have some of these things.

Blackwell accepted a position with SNCC as a voter registration worker, for which she was paid $11 every two weeks. Thus Blackwell joined the growing number of rural Mississippians—the most famous of whom was Fannie Lou Hamer (1917–1977; see box in Ella Baker entry)—providing grassroots leadership in civil rights campaigns.

Cofounds the Mississippi Freedom Democratic Party

In the summer of 1964 Blackwell participated in the formation of a new political party, the Mississippi Freedom Democratic Party (MFDP). The MFDP functioned as an alternative to the regular, all-white, Democratic Party. MFDP organizers signed up eighty thousand members and held a statewide convention in August 1964. At the convention members elected a slate of sixty-eight delegates, two of whom were Blackwell and civil rights heroine Fannie Lou Hamer. The delegates made plans to challenge Mississippi's regular Democratic Party, which excluded African Americans, at the national Democratic Party convention later that month.

At the national convention, held in Atlantic City, New Jersey, members of the MFDP claimed that they were the true representatives of the people of Mississippi, and thus should occupy Mississippi's seats on the convention floor. The convention's credentials committee, however, would not seat the MFDP. As a consolation, the committee offered the MFDP two "at-large" seats in the convention. The vast majority of the MFDP delegates, including Blackwell, rejected the offer.

Nevertheless, the MFDP drew national attention to the lack of civil rights of African Americans in Mississippi. Testimony delivered by Hamer and other MFDP delegates was influential in the passage of the Civil Rights Act of 1964, which outlawed a variety of types of discrimination based on race, color, religion, or national origin, and the Voting Rights Act of 1965, which outlawed all practices used to deny African Americans the right to vote and empowered federal registrars to register African American voters. The MFDP challenge also put an end to all-white state delegations at future national Democratic Party conventions.

In later years Blackwell served as a member of the Democratic National Committee; she was vice-chair of the Mississippi Democratic Party from 1976 to 1980.

Housing and community development activism

After the national convention, Blackwell returned to Mississippi and expanded her civil rights efforts. In 1965 she filed a landmark school desegregation lawsuit in her home county titled *Blackwell v. Issaquena County Board of Education* (although school segregation was outlawed in 1954, it was not until 1968 that significant progress was made on the integration of public schools) and worked to improve low-income housing.

In 1967 Blackwell cofounded a community development organization called Mississippi Action Community Education (MACE). The purpose of MACE was to help small settlements incorporate as towns. Legally recognized municipalities had the advantage of being able to obtain government assistance for installing electricity, paved roads, and other services. Residents of incorporated towns also had the right to elect a local government and run their own schools.

Blackwell worked with the National Council of Negro Women in the early and mid-1970s as a low-income housing coordinator. She traveled around the country, organizing groups of low-income people to work together to become homeowners. Under a Department of Housing and Urban Development program, people willing to provide maintenance and landscaping services could purchase housing units with "sweat equity." (The value of improvements made to the property would be applied to what was owed.) Under Blackwell's guidance, more than 1,500 low-income housing units were established in Gulfport, Mississippi; Puerto Rico; Dallas, Texas; and St. Louis, Missouri.

In 1973, at the invitation of actress-activist Shirley MacLaine, Blackwell traveled to China. With relations between the United States and China newly reestablished, citizens of both nations were eager for cultural exchanges. After returning from China, Blackwell cofounded the U.S.-China People's Friendship Association. Since that time she has undertaken sixteen diplomatic missions to China.

Elected mayor of Mayersville

In 1976 Blackwell was elected mayor of Mayersville, becoming the first African American woman mayor in Mississippi. Blackwell immediately put her considerable organizing experience to use, to incorporate the small town of five hundred people. Blackwell navigated the legal hurdles and incorporated Mayersville in 1978. The town began receiving $30 thousand in federal funding annually. Those funds, plus private monies raised by Blackwell, enabled the town to bring running water to every household; to pave the town's dozen roads; to purchase a fire truck; and to install a sewer system, a modest low-income housing project, and streetlights.

Blackwell also established a buying cooperative with nearby towns, through which food was purchased in bulk and parceled out to participating families. The program allowed residents to purchase food more inexpensively than they could have otherwise done. Participants in the buying cooperative were also required to perform two hours of community service.

In 1989 Blackwell was elected to head the National Conference of Black Mayors (NCBM). The NCBM, founded in 1974, is based in Atlanta, Georgia, and serves as a forum for idea-sharing and a source of technical assistance to municipalities headed by African Americans. As head of the NCBM, Blackwell brought mayors of several Chinese cities to visit the United States.

Blackwell served four terms as mayor of Mayersville. In 1993 she decided not to seek a fifth term.

Education and career in regional planning

Although Blackwell had amassed an impressive list of achievements with only an eighth grade education, she longed for more formal schooling. In 1982, at the age of fifty, Blackwell received a scholarship from the National Rural Fellows Program and was admitted to the University of Massachusetts-Amherst. The following year she completed a master's degree in regional planning, even though she had no previous college degree.

Since that time Blackwell has become a nationally recognized expert on rural housing and development. In 1994 she won the American Planning Association's Leadership Award.

Wins MacArthur genius award

In 1992 Blackwell received the prestigious "genius" award from the John and Catherine MacArthur Foundation of Chicago. The grant of $350,000, over five years, is given with no restrictions to "exceptionally gifted individuals." Blackwell, who lived modestly for many years on her $6 thousand annual salary as mayor, planned to use the award money to support herself while she wrote a book about rural community development.

Blackwell remains a committed social activist and community organizer. "You organize around the moment," she told *Essence* magazine in a 1998 interview. "You do it moment by moment, day by day, and it turns into a great work. But you don't see it at the time."

Sources

Books

"Blackwell, Unita." *Black Women in America: An Historical Encyclopedia.* Vol. 1. Edited by Darlene Clark Hine. Brooklyn, NY: Carlson Publishing, Inc., 1993: 138–39.

Crawford, Vicki L., Jacqueline Anne Rouse, and Barbara Woods, eds. *Women in the Civil Rights Movement: Trailblazers and Torchbearers, 1941–1965.* Brooklyn, NY: Carlson Publishing, Inc., 1990.

Giddings, Paula. *When and Where I Enter: The Impact of Black Women on Race and Sex in America.* New York: Bantam Books, 1984.

Robnett, Belinda. *How Long? How Long? African-American Women in the Struggle for Civil Rights.* New York: Oxford University Press, 1997.

"Unita Blackwell." *Contemporary Black Biography.* Vol. 17. Farmington Hills, MI: Gale Research, 1998, pp. 11–15.

Williams, Juan. *Eyes on the Prize: America's Civil Rights Years, 1954–1965.* New York: Penguin Books, 1987.

Articles

"Black Mayor to Receive $350,000 MacArthur Grant." *Jet.* July 6, 1992: 34.

DeRamus, Betty. "Living Legends." *Essence.* February 1999: 92+.

Gallagher, Mary Lou. "Unita Blackwell." *Planning.* March 1994: 18+.

Kilborn, Peter T. "A Mayor and Town Rise Jointly." *The New York Times.* June 17, 1992: A18.

Teltsch, Kathleen. "33 Win MacArthur Awards, Including 17 Women." *The New York Times.* June 16, 1992: A19.

John Brown

Born May 9, 1800
Torrington, Connecticut
Died December 2, 1859
Charlestown, Virginia

Abolitionist, Underground Railroad conductor, and revolutionary

"I, John Brown, am now quite certain that the crimes of this guilty land will never be purged away but with Blood."

John Brown on the day of his execution, December 2, 1859.

John Brown.
Courtesy of the Library of Congress.

In October, 1859, John Brown led twenty-one men in a raid on a federal arsenal at Harpers Ferry, Virginia. Many historians consider that incident to be the "first shots" of the American Civil War (1861–65). Brown had hoped to capture arms and ammunition, then retreat into the nearby mountains to establish a base where runaway slaves would join him for the violent overthrow of the slave system of the American South. Instead, after thirty-six hours and fifteen deaths (including two of Brown's sons), the well-planned but poorly executed revolt was crushed. Of Brown's group, ten were killed, five escaped, and the rest were hanged with their leader.

To most abolitionists Brown was a great martyr, an almost saint-like figure who gave his life in a holy crusade to end slavery. To slaveholders Brown represented a threat to their way of life. Brown's violent raid and plans of a large-scale revolt inspired southern states to stockpile arms, place greater restrictions on their slaves, and prepare for war.

Born into the cause

John Brown was born to antislavery parents, Owen and Ruth Brown, on May 9, 1800, in Torrington, Connecticut.

When John was five years old his family moved to Hudson, Ohio—a small village carved out of the wilderness about twenty-five miles south of Cleveland. The family made the long trip west by oxen-drawn wagons, taking with them their furniture and equipment, as well as their horses, cows, and other livestock.

The Browns suffered through a hard first winter in a drafty log cabin only to have their spring plantings ravaged by wild animals and a late frost. They lived on wild game and food from their neighbors. The Browns eventually adapted to life in the Ohio wilderness, making a living by farming and tanning leather. They cured the skins of rabbits, squirrels, and deer, and the hides of cattle and sheep, to produce shoes and harnesses for sale.

The Browns also made their Ohio home a stop along the Underground Railroad. They illegally sheltered runaway slaves as the slaves made their way further north or into Canada, to freedom.

Frontier life

John Brown's mother died when he was eight years old, the first of many losses he would endure throughout his life. Brown had very little formal schooling, preferring to work on the farm with his father. Most of his education was obtained by reading books from a neighbor's library.

Owen Brown sold cattle to federal troops during the War of 1812. At the age of twelve, John was given the responsibility of driving a herd of cattle over one hundred miles to the quartermaster depot. His interactions with the federal army left him with a great dislike for military affairs. When Brown came of age for military duty, he paid fines rather than enter the service.

When he was sixteen Brown traveled to Massachusetts to study to become a minister. Due to an eye infection, however, he was forced to leave school and return to Hudson. He worked at his father's tanning business and before long was made foreman of the shop. In his spare time Brown taught himself arithmetic and land surveying. At age twenty, he set up his own tannery and raised herds of sheep and cows. That year he married Dianthe Lusk and began a family.

Suffers personal and financial hardships

In 1826 Brown moved his wife and three children to northwest Pennsylvania. He built a large house and a barn with a secret room for hiding fugitive slaves, as his father had done. Brown became a leader in the small community of Randolph. He helped start a school and a post office and served as postmaster from 1828 to 1835.

In 1831, however, troubles for the Brown family began. Brown became sick and was unable to work, and one of his sons died. The following year Brown's wife died after giving birth to their seventh child. The child died a few hours later. In 1833 Brown married seventeen-year-old Mary Ann Day. In the years to come they would have seven sons and six daughters (only six of their children would live to adulthood).

In 1835 Brown, ill and with no income, moved his family back to Ohio. They settled in Franklin Mills, a village near Hudson. Brown borrowed money, established a cattle company, and began to speculate in (buy and sell) land. Seven years later, during a downturn in the nation's economy, Brown was forced to file for bankruptcy. The family then moved from one home to another as Brown took different jobs to keep them financially afloat. In Hudson Brown tried breeding racehorses. In Richfield, Ohio, he bred cattle and sheep. He twice drove herds of cattle to be sold in the East. In 1843 four of Brown's children died: three of dysentery (an infectious disease characterized by diarrhea and dehydration) and one from burns in a kitchen accident.

Throughout all his personal tragedies, Brown continued to assist with the Underground Railroad. He became increasingly intolerant of white people in the antislavery movement who only opposed slavery in word (but not in deed) and whose racism led them to treat blacks as second-class citizens.

Moves to ex-slave colony in New York

Brown began his last major business venture in 1844 as a partner in a wool operation. He moved his family to Springfield, Massachusetts, where they worked at the firm's warehouse. There Brown sought out the company of other abolitionists, especially the black leaders in the movement, whom he considered the most dedicated and principled. In 1847 Brown met **Frederick Douglass** (1817–1895; see entry), an escaped slave and one of the most eloquent champions of the abolitionist cause. The two men became close friends and confidantes. Douglass was the first person to whom Brown revealed his grand plan to raid the federal arsenal at Harper's Ferry and incite a general slave rebellion.

Brown also counted among his friends two black women, both ex-slaves, who were instrumental in the fight against slavery: **Harriet Tubman** (1820–1913; see entry), a leader of the Underground Railroad, and Sojourner Truth (1797–1883; see box in Tubman entry), a speaker and organizer for the abolitionist movement. Tubman supported Brown's plan to attack Harper's Ferry; however, when the time came she was too ill to participate in the mission.

In 1848 Brown purchased a 244-acre parcel of land in rural North Elba, New York, from his friend Gerrit Smith (1797–1874). Smith, a wealthy white abolitionist, had set aside a large tract of land in northeastern New York as a farming colony for ex-slaves and free blacks. Brown divided his time between Springfield and North Elba. In the latter location he assisted residents with their struggling farm operation and established a link on the Underground Railroad.

The fight over slavery intensifies

In 1850 Congress enacted a fugitive slave law that required federal marshals to arrest any black person accused of being a runaway slave. Arrests were made without warrant, solely on the basis of a slaveholder's assertion of ownership. The captured individual had no right to a jury trial or to give testimony in his or her own defense. Anyone caught helping a fugitive slave was subject to six months in jail and a $1,000 fine.

The new law threatened the freedom of the approximately fifty thousand runaway slaves in the North, plus the thousands of free blacks. The law essentially gave slave catchers a green light to capture any black person, regardless of their legal standing. The captors were assured handsome rewards by slaveholders willing to claim the captive as their property. Thousands of blacks—both runaway slaves and those who were legally free—immediately fled across the border to Canada.

The fugitive slave law brought the simmering battle over slavery to a full boil. White and black abolitionists defended fugitives from capture and even rescued some already in the custody of federal marshals. Brown urged his black friends in North Elba to resist the new law with violence if necessary. In Springfield Brown organized the League of Gileadites: a small group of radical whites, free blacks, and runaway slaves who pledged to fight to defend themselves and all blacks.

Bloody Kansas

The battle over slavery shifted to Kansas in the 1850s, following the establishment of Kansas as a territory in which settlers were to decide whether or not to permit slavery. Kansas's entry into the Union as a slave state would nullify the provision of the Missouri Compromise of 1820 that prohibited slavery north of the Mason-Dixon line (the boundry line between the northern and southern states). For radical abolitionists such as John Brown, the fate of Kansas was crucial in determining the fate of slavery throughout the nation.

In 1855 John Brown quit his partnership in the wool business to devote all his time and energy to fighting slavery. In June he moved his family one last time, to North Elba. In the fall of 1855, at the age of fifty-five, Brown went to Kansas to assist the antislavery movement. He joined five of his sons who had already settled there.

Brown and his followers fought many armed battles in Kansas, as well as in the bordering slave-state of Missouri, against proslavery militias. In one particularly bloody incident, in May of 1856, Brown and his group killed five proslavery settlers as revenge for their destruction of Lawrence, Kansas, a free-state town.

The antislavery forces prevailed in Kansas in August, 1858, when elections established Kansas as a free state. Brown, however, had paid a heavy personal price. One of his sons had been killed and two had been captured by the enemy (they were later released). Brown's heart was heavy but he became even more determined to wage a war against slavery. In Brown's words, he was wielding a "sword of the spirit."

In December 1858, just before leaving Kansas, Brown and ten recruits made a daring raid into Missouri. They shot and killed a slaveholder and liberated eleven slaves. Brown then personally led the slaves on an eighty-two-day, 1,100-mile journey to Canada and freedom.

The raid on Harpers Ferry

The action for which Brown is most famous was the October 16, 1859, raid on Harper's Ferry, Virginia, where there was a federal arsenal (a place to store weapons). Brown had been planning the raid for years, collecting funds from supporters, recruiting and training fighters, and stockpiling arms and ammunition. Brown planned to seize the weapons in the arsenal, then arm and incite the local slaves to rebellion.

In April 1859 members of Brown's raiding party moved into a farmhouse about five miles from Harpers Ferry. In the coming months they received secret shipments of firearms and ammunition. To keep from arousing the suspicions of his neighbors, Brown had his men keep a low profile. He moved his wife, Mary, and son, Oliver, to the farmhouse, to give the place a familial appearance.

Under cover of darkness on the morning of Sunday, October 16, Brown's group of twenty-one men, including three of his sons, headed toward Harpers Ferry. The men cut the telegraph wires leading into the town, captured the Potomac bridge, took about fifty hostages, and barricaded themselves in the armory. The decision to veer from their original plan, which was to capture arms and leave quickly, proved to be a fatal one. By the evening of the next day, about four hundred Virginia militiamen had arrived on the scene. They fired upon Brown's men, forcing them to retreat into the engine house.

The next morning a company of U.S. Marines, commanded by Robert E. Lee (1807–1870; leader of Confederate forces during the Civil War [made up of the eleven southern states that seceded from the Union]), surrounded the engine house. Brown refused to surrender. The marines stormed the building and in three minutes the battle was over. During the scuffle, one marine struck Brown in the face with a saber and another ran a bayonet through his body. Brown's men had taken heavy losses: ten lay dead (including two of Brown's sons), six (including Brown) had been captured. Only five escaped.

Tributes to John Brown

John Brown's personal sacrifices and his display of character and dignity as he faced death led some of his countrymen to publicly declare their admiration for him. "His zeal in the cause of my race was far greater than mine," commented Frederick Douglass. "I could live for the slave but he could die for him."

Noted essayist and poet Ralph Waldo Emerson (1803–1882) said that Brown's execution "made the gallows glorious like the cross."

Unitarian minister and orator Theodore Parker (1810–1860) wrote that for Brown, "The road to heaven is as short from the gallows as from a throne."

And finally, in the words of essayist and philosopher Henry David Thoreau (1817–1862): "John Brown was such a man as it takes ages to make, and ages to understand."

Sent to the gallows

As Brown lay wounded in jail awaiting his trial on charges of treason and murder, he was interviewed by two congressmen and a senator. "Why did you do it?" they asked. "To free the slaves," Brown answered. The governor of Virginia also visited Brown and had this to say about him: "They are mistaken who take [John Brown] to be a madman. He is a bundle of the best nerves I ever saw, cut and thrust and bleeding, and in bonds."

Brown was carried to his trial on a stretcher but managed to stand and tell the court, "Gentlemen, it is no use whatever to hold the mockery of a trial over me. Take me out and hang me at once!" On November 2, the jury found Brown guilty as charged and set his hanging date for December 2. On the day before he was to die, Mary Ann Brown came from North Elba to be with her husband.

On the morning of his hanging John Brown wrote a message to his countrymen and passed it to a guard at the jail. It read: "I, John Brown, am now quite certain that the crimes of this guilty land will never be purged away but with Blood."

John Brown's hanging heightened tensions between pro-slavery and antislavery forces in the United States. Seventeen months after Brown went to the gallows, the Civil War (1861–65) began. Only after the loss of 600,000 American lives was the question of slavery settled once and for all.

Sources

Books

Graham, Lorenz. *John Brown: A Cry for Freedom*. New York: Thomas Y. Crowell, 1980.

Iger, Eve Marie. *John Brown: His Soul Goes Marching On.* New York: Young Scott Books, 1969.

Meltzer, Milton. *Slavery: A World History.* Rev. edition. New York: De Capo Press, 1993.

Nelson, Truman. *The Old Man: John Brown at Harper's Ferry.* New York: Holt, Reinhart and Winston, 1973.

Oates, Stephen B. *To Purge This Land with Blood: A Biography of John Brown.* New York: Harper & Row, Publishers, 1970.

Stavis, Barrie. *John Brown: The Sword and the Word.* New York: A. S. Barnes and Company, 1970.

César Chávez

Born March 31, 1927
Yuma, Arizona
Died April 23, 1993
San Luis, Arizona

Labor leader, founder of the United
Farm Workers, and civil rights leader

"Wherever there are Mexican people, wherever there are farm workers, our movement is spreading like flames across a dry plain."

César Chávez in a speech given on April 11, 1966.

César Chávez.
Reproduced by permission of Corbis-Bettmann.

César Chávez is widely considered to have been the greatest Mexican American civil rights leader in history. Chávez brought the terrible plight of farm workers—most of whom were of Mexican descent—to the attention of the American public. He was a charismatic leader who turned the farm workers' strike into a national movement for social justice.

In the 1960s Chávez founded the United Farm Workers (UFW) union, an organization that continues to work on behalf of agricultural workers throughout the United States. While the war against injustice in the fields is far from over, Chávez's efforts have resulted in improved conditions for many farm workers.

The plight of migrant farm workers

In California's San Joaquín Valley, where the UFW originated, workers migrated from one grape harvest to the next. They performed back-breaking labor for long hours and were constantly exposed to dangerous pesticides. The average life expectancy of a farm worker in 1965 was forty-nine years; the average life expectancy of a white U.S. citizen, by comparison, was seventy years.

Farm workers typically lived in run-down one-room shacks with no heat or running water. Those who could not afford to pay for housing slept under their cars. Farm workers had little time for schooling, so most were illiterate (could not read or write). Many growers promised farm workers one wage but paid them significantly less. The typical farm worker did not speak English and thus was powerless to assert his or her rights. In the 1960s most farm workers earned less than $2 thousand per year—barely enough to survive.

Early years as a farm worker

Chávez learned about the plight of farm workers first-hand as a child. Chávez was born to a poor farming family in 1927 in Yuma, California, just before the onset of the Great Depression (the worst economic crisis ever to hit the United States, lasting from 1929 to 1939.) The Chávez family struggled to hold onto their farm through the Depression, only to be wiped out by a drought in 1937.

When Chávez was ten years old, his family began following the harvests through Arizona and California. Like other migrant children, Chávez found it difficult to attend school. He had to switch schools every time his family moved on to the next job. Chávez attended more than thirty-seven schools in all and only completed the eighth grade.

One subject young Chávez learned a lot about—both in school and out of school—was discrimination against Mexican Americans. Chávez was told in at least one school that none of the teachers wanted Mexicans in their classrooms. Most restaurants in the 1930s and 1940s refused to serve Mexican Americans or other people of color, and movie theaters had segregated seating. Mexican Americans lived in fear of brutality at the hands of police. Even while serving in the navy during World War II (1939–45), Chávez faced discrimination because of his race.

Starts a family, joins the Community Service Organization

In 1948 Chávez married his sweetheart of six years, Helena Fabel, and the two settled down in a one-room shack in Delano, California. Over the next several years, César and

Helena had eight children. Chávez worked picking cotton and grapes, hitchhiking to work and back since he had no car.

One day in 1948, the workers at Chávez's job site walked out of the fields protesting the low pay and unsafe working conditions. Most of the workers were not U.S. citizens and feared being deported (expelled from the country). Thus they ended their strike after three days, having made no gains.

Chávez was inspired by that strike. This was the first time he had seen farm workers banding together to assert their rights. To overcome the fear of deportation, Chávez began teaching the workers English so they could start the process of becoming U.S. citizens.

In 1952 Chávez met Fred Ross, founder of the Community Service Organization (CSO). The CSO, Ross explained to Chávez, was working to advance the civil rights of farm workers. Ross convinced Chávez to join the organization. Chávez began spending several hours after work each day going door-to-door, teaching people how to become U.S. citizens and how to register to vote, as well as helping them solve any number of other problems. In 1958 Chávez was promoted to the position of CSO director in California and Arizona.

The farm workers union and the grape strike

In 1962 Chávez resigned from the CSO so he could devote his energies to organizing farm workers. Chávez took the money he had saved while working for the CSO and, along with two other organizers—Dolores Huerta (1930–; see box) and Gilberto Padillo—established the National Farm Workers Association (NFWA). The leaders of the NFWA put in long hours, talking to workers in the fields about their conditions and urging them to join the NFWA. By 1965 the NFWA boasted 1,700 members.

In September 1965 the NFWA was suddenly forced to decide whether or not to go on strike. Six hundred Filipino workers of the Agricultural Workers Organizing Committee (AWOC) had gone on strike, and the growers had responded by firing the strikers and throwing them out of their homes. The Filipino workers looked to the NFWA for support. By continuing to work, the Mexican workers would hurt the Filipinos' cause. By joining the strike, they would be standing up for the rights of all farm workers.

Chávez felt that joining the strike was a risky move. His young union had no strike fund, and many NFWA members faced the possibility of losing their jobs and being deported. Nonetheless, on Mexican Independence Day, September 16, 1965, the NFWA, led by Chávez, voted to go on strike. Workers walked out of the vineyards surrounding Delano, demanding a living wage, decent housing, and humane working conditions.

Initiates grape boycott, march

Soon after the strike began, Chávez and other union leaders initiated a grape boycott. They asked the American public not to buy grapes until conditions improved for migrant workers. Students, religious leaders, labor unions, and civil rights organizations supported the farm workers. They promoted the boycott in their communities and sent the strikers food and money. People came from all over to Delano to walk on the picket lines.

To further raise the stakes, in February 1966 Chávez led the strikers on a 250-mile-long march from Delano to the California state capital of Sacramento. Twenty-one days into the march, Chávez received word that one of the largest grape-growers, the Schenley Corporation, had given in to the strikers' demands. The settlement with Schenley was the first major farm labor contract in the history of the United States.

After the settlement, the NFWA merged with the AWOC to form the United Farm Workers (UFW). The UFW chose to affiliate with the nation's largest labor conglomerate, the AFL-CIO (American Federation of Labor-Congress of Industrial Organizations). The UFW continued working to force the more than two dozen remaining growers to the table.

The marchers reached Sacramento on Easter Sunday, April 11, 1966. Chávez gave a triumphant speech on the steps of the state capitol and read from the "Plan de Delano," the document that explained the reasons behind the march.

"Now we will suffer for the purpose of ending the poverty, the misery, and the injustice," Chávez read. "This Pil-

Dolores Huerta: Chávez's Organizing Partner

Dolores Huerta (1930–) co-founded the UFW with César Chávez in 1965. Since that time Huerta has served as the union's chief negotiator, director of the national grape boycott, political strategist, and lobbyist. Undeterred by advancing age, Huerta continued to serve as secretary-treasurer of the UFW.

Huerta was born in the small mining town of Dawson, New Mexico, and at the age of five moved to Stockton, California—an agricultural community in the Central San Joaquín Valley. After completing high school in Stockton, Huerta earned a teaching degree from the University of Pacific's Delta Community College. She then took a job as an elementary school teacher. Many of Huerta's students, the children of farm workers, came to school hungry and without shoes. After a few months of teaching Huerta left her job to become a community organizer. "I thought I could do more by organizing farm workers," stated Huerta, "than by trying to teach their hungry children."

In 1952 Huerta went to work with the Community Service Organization (CSO), a civil rights organization in Los Angeles, California. It was in the CSO that she met fellow organizer Chávez. In the early 1960s Chávez tried to convince the CSO to sponsor a union for farm workers. When the CSO refused, Chávez resigned and asked Huerta to join him in organizing their own farm workers union. Huerta, a divorced mother with seven children, accepted.

grimage is witness to the suffering we have seen for generations. . . . Across the San Joaquín Valley, across California, across the entire Southwest of the United States, wherever there are Mexican people, wherever there are farm workers, our movement is spreading like flames across a dry plain. Our Pilgrimage is the match that will light our cause for all farm workers to see what is happening here, so that they may do as we have done."

Fasts for twenty-five days

By February 1968 the strike had been dragging on for two and one-half years and thousands of farm workers were still out of work. Some of the strikers began discussing committing acts of sabotage against crops and equipment. Chávez,

Dolores Huerta. *Reproduced by permission of AP/Wide World Photos.*

During the 1965 farm worker strike Huerta promoted the grape boycott on the American East Coast. When growers finally came to the bargaining table, they had to face Huerta—the UFW's chief negotiator.

Since that time, Huerta has worked tirelessly for the rights of farm workers and other oppressed people. She has testified before numerous state and national panels on the dangers of pesticides. She has also worked for the passage of major pieces of legislation that support poor people, farm workers, and immigrants, such as Aid to Dependent Children and disability and unemployment insurance for farm workers. From 1988 to 1993 Huerta served on the federal government's Commission on Agricultural Workers.

an adherent to the thoughts of Indian nationalist leader **Mohandas Gandhi** (1869–1948; see entry) and **Martin Luther King, Jr.,** (1928– 1968; see entry) claimed that the only lasting victories came by nonviolent means. To demonstrate the power of nonviolence, he began a fast on February 14.

Chávez's fast lasted twenty-five days. During that time thousands of supporters visited the room where Chávez was fasting, to speak with him, to play music for him, or just to look at him. When Chávez had lost thirty-five pounds and became too weak to walk, his doctor convinced him to break his fast.

On March 10, 1968, Chávez broke bread with Senator Robert F. Kennedy (1925–1968)—brother of assassinated president John F. Kennedy (1917–1963; president 1961–63) and an outspoken supporter of civil rights—by his side. "The world must know," said Kennedy, "that the migrant farm worker, the Mexican American, is coming into his own right."

Chávez addressed his supporters at a mass after breaking his fast. "When we are really honest with ourselves, we must admit that our lives are all that really belong to us," said Chávez. "So it is how we use our lives that determines what kind of men we are. It is my deepest belief that only by giving our lives do we truly find life. I am convinced that the truest act of courage, the strongest act of manliness . . . is to sacrifice ourselves for others."

Grape strike ends in victory

In July 1970, almost five years after the strike had begun, the remaining twenty-six nonunion Delano grape growers finally met the workers' demands. The owners' resolve had been weakened by the boycott's economic impact. The growers signed contracts granting farm workers $1.80 per hour plus twenty cents per box of grapes picked; protection against pesticides; seniority for striking workers; and a union hiring hall. The contracts covered forty thousand grape workers.

After the grape strike, Chávez and the UFW turned their attention to the plight of lettuce pickers. Here the UFW not only had to confront the growers, but another union—the Teamsters. The Teamsters had emerged as a rival to the UFW in organizing farm workers. On behalf of lettuce pickers, the Teamsters had signed contracts with a number of growers that, according to UFW leaders, were not beneficial to the workers.

The Agricultural Labor Relations Act

The battle over representation of lettuce pickers came to a head in 1975 when the California state legislature enacted the Agricultural Labor Relations Act. That legislation gave agricultural workers the right to organize and the right to determine which union would represent them. In elections held in August 1975, the workers overwhelmingly voted to join the UFW.

The UFW was never again as effective as it had been during the grape strike of the mid-1960s. Union membership declined in the 1970s and 1980s, due to many factors: competition with other unions for farm workers' membership; an inability to garner widespread support; and tighter immigration laws that resulted in a greater proportion of undocumented farm workers (the UFW only organizes workers who are in the United States legally). In the 1990s the UFW claimed about ten thousand members and held about one hundred contracts with agricultural employers.

Conducts fast to protest pesticide use

In the 1980s Chávez began a crusade against the use of dangerous pesticides in the vineyards. (Pesticides are poisonous chemicals sprayed on crops to kill insect pests or weeds. Many pesticides are hazardous to the health of humans and wildlife.) Chávez pointed out that not only did pesticides sicken farm workers but they were dangerous to grape consumers. He called upon the public to boycott grapes until the pesticides were discontinued. That boycott, however, failed to attract the widespread backing enjoyed by the original boycott.

In 1988 Chávez fasted again to protest continued pesticide use. "And the fast will endure," wrote Chávez, "until the fields are safe for farm workers, the environment is preserved for future generations, and our food is once again a source of nourishment and life."

Chávez announced an end to his fast thirty-six days after he had begun. At his side were Ethel Kennedy (Robert Kennedy's widow), his wife Helen, his mother Juana, and civil rights leader **Jesse Jackson** (1941– ; see entry).

Chávez died in April 1993 while conducting UFW business in Arizona. His funeral drew more than thirty thousand mourners, who formed a three-mile long procession to his gravesite. In August 2000 the California state legislature voted to make Chávaz's birthday, March 31, a holiday for state workers and an optional holiday for public schools.

Sources

Books

Cedeño, Maria E. *César Chávez: Labor Leader.* Brookfield, CT: The Millbrook Press, 1993.

Ferriss, Susan, and Ricardo Sandoval. *The Fight in the Fields: César Chávez and the Farmworkers Movement.* New York: Harcourt Brace & Company, 1997.

Griswold del Castillo, Richard, and Richard A. Garcia. *César Chávez: A Triumph of Sprit.* Norman: University of Oklahoma Press, 1995.

Griswold del Castillo, Richard, and Arnoldo De León. *North to Aztlán: A History of Mexican Americans in the United States.* New York: Twayne Publishers, 1996.

Levy, Jacques. *César Chávez: Autobiography of La Causa.* New York: W. W. Norton & Company, 1975.

Matthiessen, Peter. *Sal Si Puedes: César Chávez and the New American Revolution.* New York: Random House, 1969.

Mirandé, Alfredo and Evangelina Enríquez. *La Chicana.* Chicago: University of Chicago Press, 1979.

Rosales, F. Arturo. *Chicano! The History of the Mexican American Civil Rights Movement.* Houston, TX: Arte Público Press, 1997.

Articles
"California OKs Holiday for César Chávez." *Ann Arbor News* (AP). August 11, 2000: A4.

Videos
Chicano! The History of the Mexican American Civil Rights Movement. Los Angeles: NLCC Educational Media, 1996.

Web Sites
Dolores Huerta Biography. *United Farm Workers.* [Online] Available http://www.ufw.org/ (accessed February 5, 1999).

Daniel Cohn-Bendit

Born April 4, 1945
Montauban, Midi-Pyrenees, France

Social reformer and Green Party representative in the European Parliament

Daniel Cohn-Bendit has worked for more than three decades to create a utopia, or ideal society, in Europe. As a student leader in France in 1968 Cohn-Bendit drew millions of students and workers into the streets to demand everything from a shorter workweek to sexual liberation. In the 1980s Cohn-Bendit joined the German Green Party and pushed for social and environmental reforms throughout Europe. In 1999 he returned to France, the country that expelled him in 1968, and announced his intention to run for mayor of Paris in 2001.

Child of Jewish Refugees

Daniel Cohn-Bendit was born on April 4, 1945, in a town called Montauban in the south of France. His parents were German Jews who had fled their homeland in 1933 when the Nazis took power. (The Nazi Party—an abbreviation for the National Socialist German Worker's Party—was an authoritarian and anti-Semitic political party headed by Adolf Hitler.)

Cohn-Bendit's parents separated when he was a child, and his father, a prominent lawyer, moved back to Germany.

"I am not just pro-Europe, but I am a fervent believer that the construction of Europe is one of the last utopias that is left to us."

Daniel Cohn-Bendit in a 1998 interview

Daniel Cohn-Bendit.
Reproduced by permission of Archive Photos.

Paris, 1968

In May 1968 the world's eyes were on Paris, France. What began as a student protest at the suburban Parisian University of Nanterre over a policy prohibiting visitors of the opposite sex at single-sex dormitories turned into a general strike against the administration of President Charles de Gaulle (1890–1970; president of France from 1958–1968). The protesters challenged the nation's rigid ethical, cultural, sexual, and intellectual values, as well as the consolidation of power by the former war hero and army general de Gaulle.

In early May the protest spread from Nanterre to Sorbonne University, the crown jewel in France's educational system. Protesters occupied campus buildings, waving hand-lettered signs with idealistic slogans such as: "Smash the state!" "Demand the impossible," "Sex without hindrance," "Never work," and "It is forbidden to forbid." Tensions between students and police escalated. In nightly clashes on the streets, barricades were erected and cars were burned. Students pelted police with cobblestones and police struck students with billyclubs. On May 10 more than fifty protesters were hospitalized following police beatings in Paris's Latin Quarter. Televised images of police brutality generated sympathy for the protesters' cause.

Within a month's time the protest grew to include some ten million workers. A general strike by half the nation's workforce paralyzed the entire country for weeks. Factories shut down and mail,

Cohn-Bendit spent most of his youth in Paris, France, also living for periods in Germany. In 1958 Cohn-Bendit moved back to Germany with his mother and claimed German citizenship. He attended high school and college in Germany, earning a degree from the Odenwald Gymnasium in 1966.

Leads French student revolts

Cohn-Bendit next returned to Paris to study sociology at the University of Nanterre. In 1968 he led Nanterre students in opposing a school policy that prohibited visitors of the opposite sex in dormitories (which were single-sex). The students occupied campus buildings, forcing the closure of the school on May 2. As the students aired more substantial grievances about transportation, banking, and other services were suspended. De Gaulle was forced to flee the country.

At the end of May the government quelled the protests by granting major concessions to workers, such as pay raises, shorter working hours, and greater union representation in factory decision-making. When de Gaulle returned from Germany a year later, he narrowly lost a referendum on the question of his continuing presidency.

"Revolts of this type take place when politicians and society are incapable of ushering in reform," stated student leader Cohn-Bendit in an interview thirty years after the uprising. "Gaullism . . . clung to a model which was forced during [World War II] and which was marked by an authoritarianism which no longer corresponded to reality, to the concept of personal and individual freedom which had begun to predominate. So it was like a hot pot with its lid on. The explosion was inevitable."

The 1968 uprising brought about many changes in French society. In the early 1970s the voting age was lowered from twenty-one to eighteen, women won protections from discrimination in the workplace and the right to divorce, and contraception and abortion were legalized. The French left-wing (politically progressive constituency) was strengthened, paving the way for socialist candidate Francois Mitterrand to win the presidency in 1981.

university policies and social policies in general, the protests spread through the city and eventually throughout the nation (see box). "The main goals at the time (1968) were the breaking up the encrusted structures in the university, in politics, and in society," wrote Cohn-Bendit in a short online autobiography.

Cohn-Bendit, or "Danny the Red" as he was popularly known (because of both his red hair and his radical political views), was the most charismatic and visible leader of the uprising. The French government denounced him as a "German anarchist." (An anarchist is one who advocates the abolition of government in order to achieve full political liberty.)

On May 22, after what was supposed to be a short visit to Germany, Cohn-Bendit was forbidden to reenter France.

Students staged a march to protest Cohn-Bendit's expulsion. They carried signs reading "We are all German Jews," expressing their solidarity with Cohn-Bendit as well as the people victimized by Nazi forces during World War II (1939–45).

Advocates reforms in Germany

Following his expulsion from France, Cohn-Bendit moved to Frankfurt, Germany. There he founded a student group called Revolutionary Struggle (known by the initials RK, for its name in German) that called attention to the lack of affordable housing in the city. The university students in RK, together with immigrant workers, squatted (illegally occupied) housing units slated for destruction by the Frankfurt city government. Cohn-Bendit was also instrumental in establishing a system of housing cooperatives (houses and household chores shared by numerous individuals) in the city.

In the 1970s Cohn-Bendit founded a magazine in Frankfurt called *Pflasterstrand* (Pavement Beach), featuring left-wing political analysis and cultural commentary. The magazine's name came from the German translation of a slogan of the students in the 1968 Paris uprising: "Unter dem pflaster liegt der strand," which translates to "Underneath the pavement lies the beach." This slogan referred to the utopia (ideal society) they believed was being suppressed by governmental authority. At the same time, Cohn-Bendit worked in the Karl Marx Bookstore and taught kindergarten in an alternative school that emphasized personal freedoms.

Political career in the Green Party

Cohn-Bendit joined the Green Party—a political party that promoted environmentalism, women's rights, and workers' rights—in 1984 (in 1989 the party became known as the Alliance Green Party). In 1989 he was appointed by the Frankfurt city government (dominated by Greens and Social Democrats) to the honorary position of Commissioner for Multicultural Affairs. At that time large numbers of immigrants were moving to Frankfurt from Turkey, Yugoslavia, Spain, Italy, and other countries. Cohn-Bendit's commission was to assist foreigners in adjusting to life in the city and help create conditions that would foster mutual respect and acceptance among people of different ethnicities.

In a 1989 interview Cohn-Bendit discussed his new position and the question of racism in Frankfurt. "There is no virulent, militant racism in Frankfurt, but there is uncertainty," stated Cohn-Bendit. "It is hard for Germans to accept foreigners. It is not part of their tradition."

In the early 1990s Cohn-Bendit won election to the Frankfort city council and served as deputy mayor. In 1994, following the 1991 creation of the European Union (EU; organization of western European nations that works to further the joint political and economic interests of those nations), Cohn-Bendit was elected to the European Parliament (EP; the policy-making body of the EU) representing the German Green Party. Within the European Parliament he served on several committees: External Affairs, Security and Defense, and Basic Freedoms and Internal Affairs. Cohn-Bendit was also part of a group of 120 European Parliament delegates called the European Forum for Active Conflict Avoidance. The forum explores methods of nonviolent conflict resolution between nations and between factions within nations.

Returns to France

Cohn-Bendit returned to France in early 1999—this time nicknamed "Danny the Green" instead of "Danny the Red"—to head a slate of French Green Party members in that summer's EP elections. (EU regulations allow citizens of EU countries to run for EP seats anywhere in the EU.) Newspapers ran splashy headlines hailing the return to France of the fiery young man exiled more than thirty years earlier. For example, the February 1999 issue of *Europe* magazine stated: "Like the prodigal son, Daniel Cohn-Bendit is back . . . The French-born son of Jewish refugees has made a triumphant return from his political exile in Germany. Flamboyant as ever, with a mop of red hair to match his fiery temperament, he is leading France's Green Party into the European Parliament elections in June."

Cohn-Bendit handily won election to the EP representing France, becoming the first European deputy to be elected to successive five-year terms in different countries. Following the 1999 elections Cohn-Bendit applied for French citizenship and announced his intention to run for mayor of Paris in 2001.

Vision of a unified Europe

As the 1990s came to a close Cohn-Bendit continued to direct his energies toward the development of a peaceful, unified Europe. He advocated that Europe remain a strong political force, to counteract the economic dominance of the United States.

"I am not just pro-Europe, but I am a fervent believer that the construction of Europe is one of the last utopias that is left to us," stated Cohn-Bendit in a 1998 interview. "When you think that a few decades ago we were in the thick of the great wars . . . then you begin to appreciate the peace which has reigned here. Today a war between France and Germany is as unthinkable as a war between Brava and Prussia. That is progress of historical dimensions and this is the reason why I am such a fanatic for Europe. My son who is born to a hybrid father and a German mother will not have to ask himself if he will fight on the side of Germany or France. It was not the case [for] my parents."

Sources

Articles

Fisher, Andrew. "A Tamed Street Fighter: Profile, Daniel Cohn-Bendit." *Financial Times* (London). October 30, 1989.

Laushway, Ester. "Danny the Red Returns." *Europe.* February 1999: 40+.

Marlowe, Lara. "'Red' Danny gets Green Light to Contest Euro Poll." *The Irish Times.* November 17, 1998: 12.

Naravane, Vaiju. "The Revolt of May '68." *The Hindu.* May 10, 1998. Interview with Daniel Cohn-Bendit.

Tam, Pauline. "A Mellowed Danny the Red Returns." *The Gazette* (Montreal). April 17, 1999: A24.

Trueheart, Charles. "Aging and in Power 30 Years Later, Ex-Rebels Celebrate Paris Uprising." *The Washington Post.* May 25, 1998: A24.

Trueheart, Charles. "Much Politicking for Little Power: French Parties Jockeying to Gain Upper Hand in June's European Parliament Elections." *The Washington Post.* January 6, 1999: A18.

Valls-Russell, Janice. "The Legacy of May '68 in France." *The New Leader.* April 6-April 20, 1998: 7–9.

Webster, Paul. "Paris Calls Danny the Red." *The Guardian* (London). July 9, 1999: 16.

Web Sites

Cohn-Bendit, Daniel. Short Biography. *Eurospeed online.* [Online] Available http://www.oeko-net.de/eurospeed/dcbeng.htm (accessed November 4, 1999).

Barry Commoner

Born May 28, 1917
New York, New York

Environmental advocate, antinuclear activist, and research scientist

Barry Cmmoner learned about environmental devastation first-hand as a lieutenant in the U.S. armed forces during World War II (1939–45), when he participated in the spraying of the Pacific Islands with DDT (a highly toxic chemical used to kill insect pests). Since that time he has used his scientific expertise to advocate policies that protect human health and the environment. He has campaigned against nuclear weapons testing, industrial pollution, and agricultural chemicals and has pushed for the use of renewable energy (such as solar power), organic farming, and recycling. Commoner consistently argues that scientists must educate the public about the destructive potential of technological advances and that humans must learn to live in harmony with nature.

Early interest in biology

Barry Commoner was born in Brooklyn, New York, on May 28, 1917. His parents were Isidore Commoner, a Russian immigrant tailor, and Goldie Yarmolinsky Commoner. During his childhood in East New York and Flatbush (a section of New York City), Commoner demonstrated a keen interest in science. He spent his spare time scouring city parks for specimens he could examine under his microscope.

Commoner attended the prestigious James Madison High School, taking advantage of the school's strong science curriculum. After high school he enrolled in Columbia University and majored in zoology (the branch of biology dealing with animals). He paid his way through college by working odd jobs, completing a bachelor's degree with honors in 1937.

Commoner continued his studies at Harvard University in Cambridge, Massachusetts, earning a master's degree in 1938 and a doctoral degree in 1941. From 1940 through 1942 he worked as a biology instructor at Queens College.

Learns effects of pesticides in World War II

In 1942, shortly after the United States entered into World War II, Commoner joined the U.S. Naval Reserve. He was assigned to the Naval Air Force and rose to the rank of lieutenant. He was called to active duty as a science officer with the Naval Tactical Air Squadron at Patuxent, Maryland.

Commoner was involved in efforts to spray Pacific Ocean beaches with the new insecticide (chemical that kills insects) DDT. Commanders of the U.S. armed forces, concerned that U.S. troops landing on Pacific beaches may contract insect-borne diseases (such as malaria and dengue fever), had decided to spray the beaches with DDT prior to the troops' arrival. Commoner was charged with developing a sprayer to dispense the pesticide DDT and with testing the sprayer on mosquitoes on the New Jersey shore. Commoner was horrified to learn that his spraying had caused the deaths of millions of fish living in the waters off the shore. That experience was his first exposure to the environmental consequences of technology.

(After widespread use of DDT, it was established that it contaminated the environment and adversely affected the health of humans and wildlife. In humans large concentrations of DDT was found to cause liver cancer, respiratory failure, seizures, and a host of other problems of the central nervous system. The use of DDT was banned in the United States in 1972.)

From the end of the war until his discharge from the military in 1946, Commoner worked as a naval liaison to the

U.S. Senate Military Affairs Committee. In that capacity he helped establish the National Science Foundation and the Atomic Energy Commission (later renamed the Nuclear Regulatory Commission). Commoner, who was an early opponent of the use of atomic weapons, also helped coordinate Senate hearings on the atomic bomb and the Manhattan project (the secret program of the U.S. government during World War II to design and construct the world's first atomic weapons).

Areas of scientific research

In 1946, following his discharge from the military, Commoner married a psychologist named Gloria C. Gordon. The couple had two children, Lucy Alison and Frederic Gordon. From 1946 to 1947 Commoner worked as associate editor for *Science Illustrated.*

In 1948 Commoner was hired as an associate professor of plant physiology at the Henry Shaw School of Botany at Washington University in St. Louis, Missouri. He became highly regarded as a lecturer and researcher and in 1953 was promoted to the status of full professor. In 1965 Commoner was named chairman of the botany department and in 1976 was made a university professor (the highest academic designation for a faculty member) of environmental science.

Among Commoner's early research topics at Washington University was the reproduction and biochemical (chemistry of living matter) processes of the tobacco mosaic virus. This research—which had applications for the treatment of viral diseases in humans—won Commoner the prestigious Newcomb Cleveland prize of the American Association for the Advancement of Science (AAAS) in 1953. (The prize is awarded at the association's annual meeting to the young scientist who delivers the most impressive paper.)

Also in the 1950s and early 1960s, Commoner studied the roles of free radicals (molecules with unpaired electrons) in living things. Commoner and his colleagues determined that abnormal free radicals appeared at the onset of cancer in laboratory rats. The group's research proved valuable in the development of early cancer detection methods for humans.

Antinuclear weapons activism

Although enjoying a succesfulk career in biochemistry, Commoner also maintained an interest in nuclear science. In the 1950s Commoner joined forces with fellow scientist Linus Pauling (1901–1994; recipient of the Nobel Prizes for chemistry in 1954 and peace in 1962) to draw attention to the consequences of atomic-weapon testing. Commoner and Pauling drafted a petition, signed by eleven thousand scientists, that called on the United States and the Soviet Union to end their atmospheric (above-ground) testing of atomic weapons. Commoner brought the AAAS—of which he was an active member—into the atomic weapons debate as well. In 1958 he helped organize an AAAS's symposium on nuclear fallout (radioactive particles that return to earth following an above-ground detonation).

Also in 1958, Commoner spearheaded the formation of the St. Louis Committee for Nuclear Information. That committee conducted a famous study in which they convinced area residents to donate their children's baby teeth. The researchers tested the teeth and detected high levels of the radioactive strontium-90 (an element of nuclear fallout that bonds with calcium—the main component of teeth). Those results implied that radioactive elements from the nuclear tests taking place in Nevada were being absorbed into the human body at dangerous levels, at locations far downwind of the test site.

In 1963 the St. Louis Committee, which had been renamed the Committee for Environmental Information, became part of the Scientists' Institute for Public Information (SIPI). SIPI backed the international nuclear test-ban treaty—the treaty banning nuclear-weapons tests in the atmosphere, in outer space, and underwater—that was signed by the United States, the Soviet Union, and Great Britain in August 1963. Commoner served on the board of directors of SIPI from 1963 through 1980; for ten of those years he was chairman of the board.

Founds Center for the Biology of Natural Systems

In 1966 Commoner decided to limit his research to environmental issues. With a $4.25 million grant from the U.S. Public Health Service he established the Center for the

Bella Abzug: A Fighter for the Environment and Women's Rights

In 1995 Commoner shared the speaker's platform at Dartmouth College's Earth Day Conference with Bella Abzug (1920–1998)—a noted environmentalist and champion of the rights of women, African Americans, workers, poor people, and lesbians and gay men.

Abzug served in the U.S. House of Representatives from 1971 to 1976, winning election three times to represent New York's 19th District (Manhattan). Abzug's House tenure was punctuated by her opposition to the Vietnam War (1954–75) and her introduction of legislation banning discrimination against women. She also fought on the House floor for gay rights, reproductive freedoms, child welfare, and environmental protections. In 1976 she gave up her seat to run for the U.S. Senate but narrowly lost the Democratic primary to Daniel Patrick Moynihan. The next year Abzug ran for mayor of New York City, but again was defeated in the primary.

Before her tenure in the House, Abzug worked as a civil rights and labor lawyer. She often represented poor people and minorities, free of charge. Abzug first rose to fame in 1952 for representing Willie McGee, an African American in Mississippi falsely accused of raping the white woman with whom he was having an affair. McGee was found guilty by an all-white jury and sentenced to death; by filing appeals Abzug managed to delay his execution for two

Biology of Natural Systems (CBNS). The purpose of the center was to conduct research on, and train graduate students in, energy and environmental issues. A sampling of the topics that have been researched by the CBNS over the years include the occurrence of carcinogens (cancer-causing substances) in the environment, farm-based pollution, organic farming (a method of farming that does not rely on chemical-based pesticides or fertilizers), energy conservation systems for homes, solar energy, waste reduction, and the means by which dioxin (a cancer-causing chemical) is produced in incinerators.

In 1970 Commoner was pictured on the cover of *Time* magazine. The magazine called Commoner "the Paul Revere of ecology" and stated that Commoner was "endowed with a rare

Bella Abzug. *Reproduced by permission of AP/Wide World Photos.*

years. In the early 1950s Abzug also represented numerous individuals charged by Senator Joseph McCarthy of having Communist alliances.

Abzug was a regular columnist for *Ms.* magazine and authored two books: *Bella! Ms. Abzug Goes to Washington* (1972) and *Gender Gap: Bella Abzug's Guide to Political Power for American Women* (1984). She was inducted into the National Women's Hall of Fame in 1994. Abzug died on March 31, 1998, at the age of seventy-seven, from complications following heart surgery. At the time of her death she was director of the Women's Environment and Development Organization, a branch of Women USA.

combination of political savvy, scientific soundness, and the ability to excite people with his ideas."

Writes books on environmental topics

In 1966 Commoner published his first book on environmental issues. Titled *Science and Survival,* the book warned of the dangers of nuclear weapons, chemical fertilizers, gas-guzzling automobiles, and other technological developments.

Commoner's second book, *The Closing Circle,* became his most famous. The 1971 best-seller made the argument that technology has the potential to destroy human society. "Human beings have broken out of the circle of life," wrote Commoner in the book's final chapter, "driven not by biological need, but by the social organization which they have devised to 'conquer' nature. . . . The end result is the environmental crisis, a crisis of survival. Once more, to survive, we must close the circle. We must learn how to restore to nature the wealth that we borrow from it."

In 1976 Commoner published *The Poverty of Power: Energy and the Economic Crisis.* In that book he drew the connection between three crises facing the United States at the time: environmental degradation; an energy shortage; and an economic recession. He argued that the crises could only be solved together through a reshaping of priorities in modern society. That book was followed by *The Politics of Energy* in 1979, in which Commoner argued that the United States should transfer its dependence on coal and oil to alternative sources of energy (especially solar power).

Commoner's most recent book, published in 1990, is titled *Making Peace with the Planet.* In it he described a litany of environmental ills and explains how the situation has worsened since the 1960s despite huge cleanup efforts. The only cure for pollution, concludes Commoner, is to eliminate pollutants at their point of origin—in other words to create nonpolluting factories and automobiles. *Publishers Weekly,* in its review of *Making Peace with the Planet,* called the book "a blueprint of our possible future and a beacon for the environmental struggles of the '90s."

Documents incinerator-dioxin connection

In 1980 Commoner ran for president of the United States, voicing disillusionment with the platforms of the major-party candidates. He represented the Citizens Party—a newly created political organization. Commoner's campaign was largely symbolic; he garnered only one-quarter of 1 percent of the vote.

In 1981 Commoner moved back to New York City and became a professor of earth and environmental science at Queens College. He also accepted a position as visiting professor of community health at Albert Einstein College of Medicine. He remained on the faculty at Queens and Einstein Colleges until he reached the age of seventy in 1987.

In the 1980s Commoner's research was focused on garbage incinerators (machines in which large quantities of waste are burned). He found that dioxin, a compound known to cause cancer in humans, was released into the air during incineration. Commoner also developed a computer model that traced dioxin from its point of origin at incinerators, through the food chain and into the human diet. (A food chain is a transfer of food energy from one organism to another. It begins with a plant species, which is eaten by an animal species; it continues with a second animal species, which eats the first, and so on.) He argued that incineration should be stopped and that recycling should be adopted as an alternative.

Offers advice to the Russians

Following the break-up of the Soviet Union in 1991, Commoner traveled to Russia to discuss environmental issues with government officials. He was concerned that environmental safeguards may be overlooked as that country rushed toward a free-market economy. Commoner was quoted in the *New York Times* as saying that the Russians "must improve their system of production by relying on ecologically sound technologies instead of importing our mistakes."

In 1992 Commoner accepted a position as distinguished professor of industrial policy at the University of Massachusetts. The following year he was named one of ten people to be inducted into the St. Louis Walk of Fame. Inductees (all of whom had either been born in St. Louis or spent their creative years there) were honored with brass stars and bronze plaques set into the sidewalk on Delmar Boulevard in the City Loop area.

Honored on 80th birthday

In 1995, at the age of seventy-eight, Commoner was a featured speaker at the Dartmouth College Earth Day Conference (a twenty-five year commemoration of the original Earth Day). In his speech he promoted organic farming and clean-burning motor vehicles as two solutions to the environmental crisis. The same year Commoner was named as one of the "100 Who Made a Difference" by the *Earth Times*. The magazine described him as "the dean of the environmental movement, who has influenced two generations."

Commoner celebrated his eightieth birthday at a symposium held by the CBNS in his honor titled "Science and Social Action: Barry Commoner's Contribution to the Environmental Movement." Now in his eighties, Commoner continues to direct the CBNS and remains a committed environmental activist.

Sources

Books
Commoner, Barry. *The Closing Circle: Nature, Man, and Technology.* New York: Alfred A. Knopf, 1971.

"Commoner, Barry." *Current Biography Yearbook.* Edited by Charles Moritz. New York: H. W. Wilson Company, 1970, pp. 91–94.

Commoner, Barry. *Making Peace with the Planet.* New York: Pantheon Books, 1990.

Commoner, Barry. *The Poverty of Power: Energy and the Economic Crisis.* New York: Alfred A. Knopf, 1976.

Articles
Brownmiller, Susan. "CIAO Bella: Remembering Abzug, 1920–1998." *Village Voice.* April 14, 1998: 43+.

Brozan, Nadine. "Chronicle." *New York Times.* May 15, 1993: 20.

Brozan, Nadine. "Chronicle." *New York Times.* September 26, 1991: B22.

Commoner, Barry. "Recycle More and Spend Less." (Letter.) *New York Times.* July 6, 1996: 19.

Commoner, Barry. "Why Dump Recycling?" (Letter.) *New York Times.* May 29, 1991: A23.

Stuttaford, Genevieve. Review of *Making Peace with the Planet. Publishers Weekly.* March 2, 1990: 67+.

Toolan, David S. "Earth Day with Bella, Barry and Friends." *America.* May 13, 1995: 3+.

Web Sites
"Bella Abzug: 1920–1998." The National Women's Hall of Fame. [Online] Available http://www.greatwomen.org/abzug.htm (accessed November 1, 1999).

Mairead Corrigan
Born January 27, 1944
Belfast, Northern Ireland

Betty Williams
Born May 22, 1943
Belfast, Northern Ireland

Northern Irish peace activists

Mairead Corrigan and Betty Williams came of age at a time when their homeland—Northern Ireland—was beset by armed struggle between the Irish Republican Army (IRA) and factions loyal to Great Britain. Corrigan and Williams were brought together when, as a result of the conflict, three children were killed: Williams witnessed the tragedy, and Corrigan was related to the victims. The two women established an organization called the Community of Peace People and pledged to bring an end to the violence. The efforts of Corrigan and Williams, which have been credited with cutting in half the death toll in Northern Ireland, earned the two women the 1976 Nobel Peace Prize.

Corrigan and Williams won the 1976 Nobel Peace Prize for their efforts to bring about peace in war-torn Northern Ireland.

Corrigan's Catholic working-class roots

Mairead (pronounced mah-RADE; Irish for Margaret) Corrigan was born on January 27, 1944, to a West Belfast Catholic working-class family. She was the second child of seven—five girls and two boys. She attended a Catholic school until the age of fourteen, at which time she was forced to leave

Mairead Corrigan (left) and Betty Williams (right).
Reproduced by permission of AP/Wide World Photos.

Roots of Northern Ireland's Conflict

Northern Ireland came into existence in 1921, when the northern section of Ireland was partitioned from the rest of the island. The Republic of Ireland (the larger southern and mainly Catholic region) was allowed to govern itself while Northern Ireland remained a part of the United Kingdom (the U.K. also includes England, Scotland, and Wales).

Northern Ireland's Catholic minority (Protestants formed the majority) complained of being brutalized by the police and of being discriminated against in terms of welfare, social benefits, and public employment. The Catholics advocated the reunification of Northern Ireland with the Irish Republic.

Unable to reach a political solution, some Catholics in Northern Ireland—led by the Irish Republican Army (IRA)—attempted to rectify the situation through military means. Protestants formed their own armed groups, such as the Ulster Volunteer Force, the Ulster Defense Association, and the Ulster Freedom Fighters, and retaliated against the IRA by assassinating Catholic activists. In 1969 English soldiers were sent into Northern Ireland to suppress the growing Catholic rebellion and maintain order. To the Catholic community, the English forces were an occupying army.

After the English troops arrived, the violence only escalated. By the mid-1970s Northern Ireland—a region in which homicide was previously nearly nonexistent —was experiencing two hundred killings a year.

because her parents could no longer afford tuition. Corrigan next went to junior college to learn clerical skills, after which she worked as a secretary for a manager at the Guinness Brewing Company.

As a young adult, Corrigan was not politically active. Her social involvement was limited to volunteering for a Catholic welfare organization called the Legion of Mary. In that capacity she supervised youth recreational activities in poor areas of West Belfast and visited prisons to discuss spiritual matters with inmates. Corrigan feared both the British soldiers patrolling her streets and the Irish Republican Army (IRA) militants opposing them (see box). She was opposed to the use of violence on both sides of the conflict.

Williams's mixed-religion heritage

Betty Williams came from a family of mixed religions: her father was Protestant, her mother was Catholic, and her grandfather had been a Polish Jew. Williams was born on May 22, 1943, and grew up in a Catholic area of Belfast known as Andersonstown. When Williams was thirteen her mother suffered an incapacitating stroke, leaving Williams in charge of raising her younger sister. Like Corrigan, Williams attended Catholic schools and took secretarial courses.

At the age of eighteen Williams married an engineer in the merchant marine, an English Protestant named Ralph Williams. They traveled extensively because of Williams's job in the merchant marines. The couple had a son and a daughter, and Williams worked intermittently as an office receptionist.

As a young adult, Williams was sympathetic to the aspirations of the Irish Republicans—in particular, an end to British oppression and a reunion of Northern Ireland with the Republic of Ireland (see box for details). As she aged, however, she came to oppose violence in all forms. In 1972 Williams joined a peace organization headed by a Protestant clergyman.

Pair united by tragedy

The lives of Corrigan and Williams intersected on August 10, 1976, when both were affected by the same tragedy. Williams witnessed a car careen out of control and strike and kill three children and seriously injure the children's mother. The pedestrians who were struck happened to be Corrigan's sister and her children. The car had gone off of the road because its driver—a member of the IRA (see box)—had been shot and killed by British soldiers pursuing the vehicle.

Corrigan appeared on television with her brother-in-law, Jackie Maguire, and condemned the IRA for instigating violence in the area. Williams, for her part, went door-to-door in Catholic areas of Belfast collecting more than six thousand signatures on a petition calling for peace.

Corrigan and Williams first came face-to-face at the funeral for the Maguire children. The duo decided to continue their efforts for peace and formed an organization called Women for Peace. Shortly thereafter, Corrigan and Williams—

with a newspaper reporter named Ciaran McKeown—renamed the group Community of Peace People.

Community of the Peace People holds demonstrations

Corrigan and Williams immediately set to work organizing their first peace march. They attracted a mixed Catholic-Protestant group of ten thousand people to walk to the graves of the Maguire children. Sinn Fein (pronounced shin fain), the political wing of the IRA, condemned the march and called the new organization "one-sided and deceptive." Activists from both the IRA and the Ulster forces showed up along the parade route and accused marchers of "selling out" or "collaborating with the enemy." Some marchers, including Corrigan and Williams, were physically assaulted.

The Peace People sponsored two more peace marches before the end of August. At the third such event, a group of more than thirty thousand Catholics and Protestants marched together between two rival sections of Belfast, Northern Ireland: the Falls area (mostly Catholic) and the Shankill Road area (mostly Protestant). Throughout the rest of the year, the Peace People sponsored regular peace demonstrations elsewhere in Northern Ireland, as well as in Dublin (Republic of Ireland) and London, England. Corrigan and Williams persevered despite receiving numerous death threats and gained international sympathy for their cause.

Awarded Nobel Peace Prize

Corrigan and Williams's work won them a nomination for the Nobel Peace Prize in 1976. The Nobel committee, however, delayed making an award that year. In the meantime, newspapers and civic organizations in Norway (the country that hosts the Nobel committee) kept up the campaign on Corrigan and Williams's behalf and helped solicit more than $300,000 in donations from around the world. The money was spent on joint Catholic-Protestant projects and activities, as well as repairs to factories and schools that had been damaged in bombings. The money was also used for loans to small businesses in embattled areas of Northern Ireland.

In 1977 the two women were belatedly granted the 1976 Nobel Peace Prize. Williams, in accepting the award, spoke about the responsibility of women in bringing about peace: "The voice of women has a special role and a special soul-force in the struggle for a nonviolent world. We do not wish to replace religious sectarianism or ideological division with sexism or any kind of militant feminism. But we do believe . . . that women have a leading role to play in this great struggle."

Also in 1977 Corrigan and Williams were granted honorary doctorates from Yale University in New Haven, Connecticut, and the Carl von Ossietzky Medal for Courage from the Berlin chapter of the International League for Human Rights. In a 1977 interview Corrigan stressed the role of education in eliminating the tensions between rival factions in Northern Ireland. "Unfortunately we never question our educational system," stated Corrigan. "If we stop to evaluate a lot of our old ideas and concepts, we find that they're myths, that they're false; and that bigotry has created the fear and hatred that divides our peoples."

Controversy plagues the movement

By 1978 enthusiasm for the Community of Peace People had begun to wane. In addition, some members were accusing Corrigan and Williams of getting rich off the movement (both women, who had quit their jobs to devote all their time to the movement, were being paid with Peace People funds). In the interest of saving the organization, Corrigan and Williams resigned as chairpersons but remained active members within the organization.

At the same time, the Community of Peace People shifted its emphasis from large-scale demonstrations to small-scale projects within beleaguered communities. For instance, the group funded improvements to youth recreational facilities, held interfaith discussions, and continued to assist small businesses.

Beyond the Peace People

In the early 1980s Corrigan and Williams parted ways. Corrigan's life underwent a shift in 1980 when her sister Ann Maguire, having lost her three children four years earlier, committed suicide. In 1981 Corrigan married Jackie Maguire, her former brother-in-law, and helped him raise his two surviving children (Corrigan and Maguire also had one son together). Corrigan remained active with the Peace People and traveled around the world delivering her message of nonviolence.

In 1982, her first marriage having ended in divorce, Williams married a teacher named James T. Perkins. The couple had one daughter. Four years later the Williams-Perkins family moved to Florida. There Williams became active in the movement to freeze production of nuclear weapons and to abolish the death penalty. She also wrote children's fiction.

Impact of the Northern Irish peace movement

While the Peace People's series of peace marches was short-lived, the organization's contribution toward attaining peace in the region was considerable. One indicator was that the average yearly number of killings in Northern Ireland each year was reduced from its pre-1976 level of two hundred to less than one hundred since that time.

In the mid-1990s a peace process in Northern Ireland was begun, with discussions involving the governments of England, the Republic of Ireland, and Northern Ireland, as well as Sinn Fein. A cease-fire, adhered to by all parties except one of the Ulster groups, was announced in 1994. In 1998 every political party in Northern Ireland endorsed the Northern Ireland Peace Agreement (also called the Good Friday Agreement), giving Catholics greater rights while maintaining Northern Ireland's ties with England. Despite that agreement, episodes of political violence continued to plague Northern Ireland.

"The Community of Peace People believes that the missing link in the peace process is the right of the Northern Irish people themselves to define what they want and how to achieve it," stated Corrigan in a 1994 interview. "When the Peace People started in 1976, our main message was that violence is not working, be it paramilitary or state violence. . . . Second, we said that only if the two traditions [Catholics and Protestants] in the North of Ireland work together . . . can they solve their problem. . . . The peace process is really up to the people; we are the only ones who can deliver real constitutional stability."

Sources

Books

Abrams, Irwin. "Corrigan, Mairead; Williams, Betty." In *Protest, Power, and Change: An Encyclopedia of Nonviolent Action from ACT-UP to Women's Suffrage.* Edited by Roger S. Powers and William B. Vogele. New York: Garland Publishing, Inc., 1997.

Buscher, Sarah, and Bettina Ling. *Máiread Corrigan and Betty Williams: Making Peace in Northern Ireland.* New York: The Feminist Press of the City of New York, 1999.

Deutsch, Richard. *Mairead Corrigan, Betty Williams.* Translated by Jack Bernard. Woodbury, NY: Barron's Educational Series Inc., 1977.

Gay, Kathlyn, and Martin K. Gay, eds. *Heroes of Conscience: A Biographical Dictionary.* Santa Barbara, CA: ABC-CLIO, 1996, pp. 93–95.

Articles

Keerdoja, Eileen. "Ulster's Peace Women." *Newsweek.* March 27, 1978: 18.

Reed, Roy. "Two Battlers for Peace: Mairead Corrigan and Betty Williams." *New York Times.* October 11, 1977.

Schroeder, Steven. "Toward a Higher Identity: An Interview with Mairead Corrigan Maguire." *The Christian Century.* April 20, 1994: 414+.

Web Sites

Engle, Dawn, and Ivan Suvanjieff. "An Interview with Mairead Corrigan Maguire." [Online] Available http://www.peacejam.org/peacejam/maguire/interview.html (accessed March 19, 2000).

Angela Davis

**Born January 26, 1944
Birmingham, Alabama**

Social activist, educator, author, and social historian

"Homelessness, unemployment, drug addiction, and illiteracy are only a few of the problems that disappear from public view when the human beings contending with them are relegated to cages."

Angela Davis

A ngela Davis grew up on Birmingham's (Alabama) "dyna-mite hill"—an African American neighborhood named because of the frequent bombings there by white supremacists. Davis's exposure to racism in her youth led to her involvement in antiracist causes as she grew older. After going to college in Massachusetts and abroad, she moved to the U.S. West Coast and became involved in civil rights and black-power organizations and the Communist Party.

In 1970 Davis was charged with conspiracy relating to a courtroom shooting incident. She fled from the law and was placed on the FBI's Ten Most Wanted list. After her capture Davis spent one and one-half years in jail awaiting trial. She was eventually cleared of all charges. Today Davis is a professor of the history of consciousness at the University of California-Santa Cruz. She remains a fighter for women's rights and a critic of the United States's criminal justice system.

Childhood in the segregated South

Davis was born on January 26, 1944, in Birmingham Alabama. Her mother, Sallye E. Davis, was a schoolteacher. Her father, B. Frank Davis, was a teacher by training but had given up the profession because of its low pay. Instead, he ran a gas station and repaired cars. The middle-class African American neighborhood in which Davis, her three younger siblings, and her parents lived was called "dynamite hill"—a nickname owed to the frequency of bombings by members of the Ku Klux Klan (a white supremacist organization known for its intimidation and acts of violence against African Americans and members of other racial and ethnic minorities).

Davis attended segregated (separated by race, as dictated by law) schools. Her classes were held in run-down buildings and her textbooks were hand-me-downs from white schoolchildren. Davis and her classmates were taught that their future success depended upon their hard work, but no mention was made of the obstacles that racism would place in their path.

Davis's greatest influence during her youth was her mother. Sallye Davis was a social activist and a great believer in education. She had protested the imprisonment of the Scottsboro boys (nine African American youths falsely accused of rape in Alabama in 1931) and let Angela accompany her to civil rights demonstrations in downtown Birmingham in the early 1950s. Angela Davis spent the first two summers of her high school years in New York City, where her mother was working toward a master's degree at New York University.

Completes high school in New York

Davis was an "A" student at her Birmingham high school but found her courses unstimulating. She was treated to a much more challenging education for her final two years of high school, at New York City's Elizabeth Irwin High School. Davis's education at the private New York school was financed by the **American Friends Service Committee**, a Quaker-based peace and justice organization (see entry). Elizabeth Irwin, located in Greenwich Village, was staffed by teachers who had been barred from employment in the public schools because of their leftist (politically progressive) points of view. At Elizabeth Irwin, Davis was introduced to the ideology of socialism (the belief that the means of production should not be controlled by owners, but by the community as a whole) and joined a socialist political organization called Advance.

Studies philosophy in college

After graduating from high school in 1961 Davis continued her schooling at Brandeis University in Waltham, Massachusetts. She studied French literature for two years, then spent a year abroad at the celebrated Sorbonne University in Paris, France. Davis's education in Paris went beyond academics—she also learned about the effects of colonialism and oppression. From conversations with students from Algeria, in Africa, Davis learned about France's previous domination of that nation and the Algerian people's struggle for independence (which they won in 1962). During her year abroad Davis learned that four girls she had known in Birmingham were killed in the bombing of the Sixteenth Street Baptist Church (September 15, 1963).

Davis returned to Brandeis for the 1964–65 academic year and studied with Marxist (adherent of the teachings of German revolutionary socialist thinker **Karl Marx**, 1818–1883; see entry) philosopher Herbert Marcuse (1898–1979). The German-born Marcuse, who had fled to the United States when the Nazis (authoritarian party headed by Adolf Hitler) rose to power in Germany, was noted for his critique of modern society—especially what he viewed as the substitution of material goods for fundamental freedoms.

After graduating from Brandeis in 1965, Davis spent two years studying philosophy in Frankfurt, Germany, with Marcuse's former teaching colleagues Theodore Adorno (1903–1969) and Oskar Negt. Both Adorno and Negt claimed that Davis was the best student they had ever taught.

Political activism on West Coast

In 1967 Davis enrolled in a graduate program at the University of California-San Diego (UC-San Diego) and once again studied under Marcuse. (Marcuse had accepted a teaching position there following his retirement from Brandeis.) While Davis had enjoyed her time in Germany, she was anxious to get back to the United States and participate in the civil rights and black power movements she had been hearing so much about. (Black power was the social movement and rallying cry of radical African American activists in the mid-1960s through mid-1970s. To many African Americans, "black power" stood for racial pride and the belief that African Americans held the power to create a better society for themselves.)

In California Davis jumped right into the social protest scene. She worked with the Black Students Council at UC-San Diego and helped found an alternative college for minority students. Davis also participated in a black-power group called the San Diego Black Conference. At a 1967 meeting sponsored by the civil rights group **Student Nonviolent Coordinating Committee** (SNCC; see entry) in Los Angeles, California, Davis met people involved with SNCC, the **Black Panther Party** (an organization founded by African American activists that opposed police abuse and provided social services to community members; see entry), and the Communist Party.

In 1968 Davis moved to Los Angeles and joined SNCC and the Panthers. Soon, however, she became disillusioned with the sexism she found in those groups (in her experience, women did most of the work while men gave orders and took all the credit). Davis left those groups and joined the Communist Party—an organization in which she found people who shared her views on the liberation of women, people of color, and poor people.

New teaching career becomes embroiled in controversy

Davis obtained her master's degree in philosophy in 1969 and by 1970 had completed all the requirements for her doctoral degree except her dissertation. Davis was hired as a lecturer by the University of California-Los Angeles in 1969 and taught four classes on philosophy and African American literature. She gained an instant following among students.

In July 1969 Davis's affiliation with the Communist Party was made public. Despite the popularity of her classes, the University of California (UC) Board of Regents—with the backing of then-governor Ronald Reagan—revoked her teaching appointment. Davis fought the termination in court, claiming a constitutional right to freedom of association and freedom of expression. She was victorious and regained her teaching position.

The UC regents' determination to get rid of Davis only increased throughout the 1969–70 academic year. During that time Davis became famous as an impassioned defender of three prisoners known as the Soledad Brothers (see below). In

June 1970 the regents terminated Davis's employment on the grounds that she had made "inflammatory" and "improper" comments in public and had not completed her doctorate.

Defends the Soledad Brothers

In 1970 Davis stood at the center of a campaign for justice for three prisoners known as the Soledad Brothers. The three men—Fleeta Drumgo, John Cluchette, and George Jackson—were African American inmates at the maximum-security Soledad Prison in Salinas, California. They had been charged with the death of a white guard in their housing unit (the guard had been beaten and thrown over a third-floor railing following another white guard's shooting of four prisoners in the prison yard just days earlier). Every inmate in the unit was confined to his cell, and Drumgo, Cluchette, and Jackson—known in the prison for their radical politics and involvement with the **Black Panther Party** (see entry)—were accused of the crime. A grand jury, in secret proceedings, indicted the men despite the lack of evidence against them.

When word of the trumped-up charges leaked out, activists and lawyers rushed to the three men's defense. Davis was outraged by the injustice in the case, especially upon learning that Jackson had served nine years in prison, seven of them in solitary confinement, for stealing $70 from a gas station. Davis became cochair and spokesperson for the Soledad Brothers defense committee. Through a series of letters and two meetings, Davis developed a close emotional bond with Jackson.

Makes FBI's Ten Most Wanted list

In August 1970 Davis went from prisoner-rights activist to fugitive. The source of her trouble was four guns she had legally purchased for her own defense (Davis had received numerous death threats as a result of her high-profile position in the Soledad Brothers' case). The guns were somehow obtained and used by Jonathan Jackson, the younger brother of George Jackson. Jonathan Jackson carried with him Davis's guns on August 7, 1970, when he stormed into the Marion County courthouse, attempted to free a prisoner on trial, took hostages, and fled. The incident resulted in the deaths of four people—Jackson, a judge, and two inmates.

Books by Angela Davis

Davis began her career as an author in 1971 when she collaborated with the Soledad Brothers and other activists on *If They Come in the Morning: Voices of Resistance.* The book addressed the unfairness of the criminal justice system toward people of color. In 1974 Davis published *Angela Davis: An Autobiography,* which focused on her embrace of communism (a system in which production and goods are commonly owned), her time in prison, and her work with political prisoners.

The following decade Davis authored *Women, Race and Class* (1983) and *Women, Culture and Politics* (1989).

The first book traces the development of feminism throughout history, while the second looks at issues of race and class in American culture and social movements.

The year 1998 saw the publication of *Blues Legacies and Black Feminism: Gertrude "Ma" Rainey, Bessie Smith, and Billie Holiday.* In that book Davis explained how those women blues singers gave early expression to women's issues and created a social history of African Americans. As the 1990s wound to a close Davis was at work on a book called *Dispossession and Punishment,* a critique of the expanding prison system and its impact on people of color in the United States.

When the Federal Bureau of Investigation (FBI) learned that the guns used by Jackson were registered to Davis, they issued a warrant for her arrest. Davis went into hiding, fearing that she would not be treated fairly. The state of California charged Davis with kidnapping, conspiracy, and murder, and the FBI placed her on its Ten Most Wanted list. (Under California law, a person who is considered to be an accessory to a crime is treated as the person suspected of actually committing the crime.)

Davis remained in hiding for two months, during which time the FBI conducted an internationally publicized manhunt. Davis was finally captured in a New York motel room. She was brought back to California and jailed without bail. Her imprisonment became a cause célèbre and the cry "Free Angela" reverberated in street demonstrations from Los Angeles to Sri Lanka. The low point of Davis's time in jail came on August 21, 1971, when she learned that George Jackson had been killed in an alleged escape attempt.

On June 4, 1972, following one of the most closely watched trials in history, Davis was acquitted of all charges by a jury of eleven whites and one Mexican American. She then organized the constituents of the "Free Angela" movement into a new a political organization called the Alliance Against Racist and Political Repression.

Resumes teaching career

After Davis's trial, even though she was cleared of all charges, the University of California regents refused to rehire her. In 1975 Davis found employment at Claremont College in Claremont, California, and in the following years at a series of California schools including Stanford University, California College of the Arts and Crafts, San Francisco State University, and San Francisco Art Institute. She also taught courses at Moscow University in Russia and Havana University in Cuba.

In 1991 Davis reentered the University of California system as a professor in the "history of consciousness" graduate program at UC-Santa Cruz. In 1995 she received a prestigious appointment as presidential chair, in which capacity she was authorized to develop new ethnic studies courses.

Activism in the 1980s and 1990s

After her period of fiery activism in the 1970s, Davis settled into a calmer—but no less committed—life of social activism. She continued her involvement with the Communist Party, running as its vice-presidential candidate in U.S. presidential elections in 1980 and 1984. In the 1980s Davis joined the leadership of the National Political Caucus of Black Women and the National Black Women's Health Project.

In the 1990s Davis championed such causes as the rights of people with AIDS, abortion rights, women's rights, and prisoner rights. As the millennium drew to a close Davis turned her attention to the expanding prison system—what she calls the prison industrial complex. Davis contends that the warehousing of greater numbers of people, for increasing lengths of time, is destroying society and is disproportionately affecting people of color.

"Almost two million people are currently locked up in the immense network of U.S. prisons and jails," stated Davis in a 1998 interview. "More than 70 percent of the imprisoned population are people of color. . . . Imprisonment has become the response of first resort to far too many of the social problems that burden people ensconced in poverty. These problems are often veiled by being conveniently grouped together under the category 'crime.' . . . Homelessness, unemployment, drug addiction, and illiteracy are only a few of the problems that disappear from public view when the human beings contending with them are relegated to cages."

Sources

Books

Churchill, Ward, and Jim Vander Wall. *Agents of Repression: The FBI's Secret War Against the Black Panther Party and the American Indian Movement.* Boston: South End Press, 1988.

Davis, Angela. *Angela Davis: An Autobiography.* Rev. ed. New York: Random House, 1990.

"Davis, Angela (Yvonne)." *Current Biography.* Edited by Charles Moritz. New York: W. W. Wilson Company, 1972, pp. 97–101.

Davis, Angela. *Women, Race and Class.* New York: Random House, 1981.

Davis, Angela. *Women, Culture and Politics.* New York: Random House, 1989.

Giddings, Paula. *When and Where I Enter: The Impact of Black Women on Race and Sex in America.* New York: Bantam Books, 1984.

Nadelson, Regina. *Who Is Angela Davis? The Biography of a Revolutionary.* New York: Peter H. Wyden, Inc., 1972.

Articles

Beyette, Beverly. "Angela Davis Now; On a Quiet Street in Oakland, the Former Radical Activist Has Settled in but not Settled Down." *Los Angeles Times.* March 9, 1989: 1.

Colby, Michael. Review of *Blues Legacies and Black Feminism: Gertrude "Ma" Rainey, Bessie Smith, and Billie Holiday. Library Journal.* February 15, 1998: 144.

Gordon, Avery F. "Globalism and the Prison Industrial Complex: An Interview with Angela Davis." *Race and Class.* October 1998: 145+.

Wallace, Amy. "Angela Davis Again at Center of UC Storm." *Los Angeles Times.* February 20, 1995: A3.

Weathers, Diane, and Tara Roberts. "Kathleen Cleaver and Angela Davis: Rekindling the Flame." *Essence.* May 1996: 82+.

Dorothy Day

Born November 8, 1897
Brooklyn, New York
Died November 29, 1980
Brooklyn, New York

Social service provider, peace activist, editor, and religious worker

Day founded the *Catholic Worker* newspaper and the nationwide social movement of the same name. She was motivated by her religious faith to work for a more caring society.

Dorothy Day.
Public Domain.

Dorothy Day remains one of the most highly regarded social activists in the history of the United States. After converting to Catholicism, she lived a life of voluntary poverty and community service. Since the 1930s the Catholic Worker movement Day founded has provided relief to untold numbers of poor and homeless people. Day's dedication to peace was unfailing; she protested armed conflict during two world wars and encouraged draft card burning during the Vietnam War (1954–75). In the wake of Day's death there has been a campaign to canonize her as a saint.

Daughter of a journalist

Day was born on November 8, 1897, in Brooklyn, New York. When she was six years old her family moved to San Francisco, California, where her father, a journalist, was offered a job covering horse races. The family lived in San Francisco until the 1906 earthquake destroyed the city.

The Days then moved to Chicago, Illinois. Work and money were scarce. The family lived in a small apartment above a saloon in a poor section of town. They had little to eat besides potato soup, bananas, tea, and bread.

Embraces socialism and writing

Day did well in school and, following her father's example, showed a talent for writing. She was awarded a scholarship by Hearst newspapers to attend the University of Illinois. There Day met people involved in communist and socialist groups. (Communism is a political system in which the government controls all resources and means of producing wealth; socialism is social and economic organization based on the control of the means of production by the community as a whole, rather than by individuals or private corporations.) Her best friend, a Jewish woman named Rayna Simons, was a member of the Communist Party. Day herself joined a socialist organization and a writers' club.

After her sophomore year, Day dropped out of college and moved to New York City. There she found kinship with a group of radical thinkers and bohemians (people, such as writers or artists, who have an unconventional lifestyle) in Greenwich Village, among them revolutionary journalists **John Reed** (1887–1920; see entry), Leon Trotsky (1879–1940), and Max Eastman (1883–1969). Eastman, who edited the radical political and literary journal *The Masses,* invited Day to write for the paper. *The Masses* took a strong stance against United States involvement in World War I (1914–18). In 1918, just six months after Day came on board, the paper was shut down under the 1917 Espionage Act, and Eastman was brought to trial for treason (the jury was unable to come to a unanimous decision, and the case was thrown out).

Day was also arrested during that period for her participation in a suffrage protest. She was one of forty women who picketed the White House demanding the right of women to vote. The women were freed after staging a hunger strike. (Women were granted the right to vote in 1920 with the passage of the Nineteenth Amendment.) Day would go to jail seven more times throughout her life for social causes.

Writes autobiographical novel

In 1919 Day began writing a novel, called *The Eleventh Virgin,* with themes that mirrored her own life. In 1924 Day's novel was published and the movie rights sold to a Hollywood, California, producer for a large sum of money. Day bought a beach house on Staten Island, New York, and lived there with Forster Batterham, a biology teacher with whom she had entered into a common-law marriage. (Batterham was opposed to the legal institution of marriage, which he viewed as government control over people's private lives.)

Batterham was an anarchist (one who advocates the abolition of government, to achieve full political liberty) and an atheist (one who denies the existence of God). Day, in contrast, was moving toward embracing Christianity. The couple frequently clashed over the topic of religion during their four-year relationship.

Birth of daughter leads Day to embrace religion

On March 3, 1927, Day gave birth to a baby girl— Tamar Theresa Day. Day was so overcome with emotion at her daughter's birth that she felt the experience was a miracle. That feeling inspired Day to have her daughter baptized in the Catholic Church.

In December of the following year Day herself was baptized. At the same time, Day's relationship with Batterham came to an end. Day strove from that point onward to reconcile her religious faith with her radical social ideals.

Day spent the next five years traveling with her daughter and trying to make a living as a writer. She wrote screenplays in Hollywood, covered political happenings in Mexico, and reported on events during the Great Depression (the worst economic crisis ever to hit the United States, from 1929 to 1939). Day was particularly affected by the poverty, hunger, and homelessness she witnessed throughout the United States during the Depression's early years.

Cofounds *Catholic Worker* with Maurin

In 1932 Day had a fateful meeting with a Frenchman named Peter Maurin. Like Day, Maurin was a radical Catholic and a writer. Day described Maurin, in her biography by William Miller, as "a genius, a saint, an agitator, a writer, a lecturer, a poor man, and a shabby tramp, all in one." Maurin had been sent to Day's home by the editor of *Commonweal* (a faith-based news journal for which both Day and Maurin wrote). The editor had believed, correctly, that Day and Maurin would have a lot in common.

Maurin felt that society was being destroyed by materialism and greed, and that the cure for society's ills lay in farming, spirituality, and knowledge. He advocated voluntary poverty, pacifism, and communal living. He felt it was the responsibility of himself and others who shared his vision to feed the hungry and shelter the homeless. Day, for one, shared Maurin's vision.

In order to spread their message and offer Catholic solutions to social problems, Day and Maurin founded a newspaper called the *Catholic Worker*. They produced the first issue on Day's kitchen table and sold it, for a penny a copy, at a May Day (holiday honoring workers) parade and rally at New York's Union Square in 1933. In the first edition, Day wrote: "The fundamental aim of most radical sheets is the conversion of its readers to radicalism and atheism. . . . Is it not possible to protest, to expose, to complain, to point out abuses and demand reforms without desiring the overthrow of religions?"

By the end of its first year of publication, the weekly *Catholic Worker* had a circulation of one hundred thousand. In 1936, at its peak, the paper sold 150,000 copies. Day maintained editorial control over the paper until slowed by old age in the late 1970s. She consistently advocated simple living and personal acts of compassion, and denounced militarism, capitalism, and communism (she felt the latter two forms of government both robbed individuals of their dignity).

Catholic Worker hospitality houses

The *Catholic Worker* newspaper sparked a social movement by the same name. Catholic Worker houses—communal dwellings (in which groups of people share the maintenance and expenses of the household) similar to one Day and Maurin had opened in Brooklyn, New York—sprung up around the nation, as did Catholic Worker communal farms. These religious people, who were committed to social change and acts of charity, set up housekeeping and provided food, shelter, and clothing to poor people.

Investigated by the FBI

Day and her Catholic Worker movement came under intense scrutiny by the Federal Bureau of Investigation (FBI) more than once. The group was first investigated during World War II (1939–45) when Day took the unpopular position of opposing the war. Many of Day's followers even deserted her at that time, believing that U.S. involvement was crucial to stopping Adolf Hitler's (1889–1945) murderous regime. Day, however, was unyielding in her pacifistic beliefs. The FBI was also suspicious of Day because of her links to communists and socialists in the past. After a four-year investigation, however, they closed her file. Day was characterized by the FBI as "pacifist and anti-Communist."

Day's FBI file was reopened during the Cold War (a period of tense relations between the United States and the former Soviet Union, from 1945 to 1990) in the 1950s. Day opposed the U.S. government's militaristic approach to the political stand-off—particularly the preparations for nuclear war. Day urged people not to participate in air-raid drills (exercises in which people would respond to sirens by taking cover, as they were to do in the event a bomb was actually dropped) or register for the draft. Again, however, the FBI failed to make a case that Day was a threat to national security.

"Keeping Out of War." Dorothy Day (center).
Reproduced by permission of Corbis Corporation (Bellevue).

The Catholic Workers lived humbly, subsisting on small contributions by individuals or churches. As a matter of principle, they refused funding from the government and corporations. "How we pay our bills I do not know," remarked Day in 1975, after her house had been operating for forty years. "God knows."

Many prominent activists either lived in or were influenced by the Catholic Worker movement—among them Tomas Merton (monk and social critic, 1915–1968), Michael Harrington (socialist activist, educator, and author, 1928–1989), and **César Chávez** (labor leader, 1927–1933; see entry).

According to the Catholic Worker site on the Internet, "Today over 140 Catholic Worker communities remain committed to nonviolence, voluntary poverty, prayer, and hospitality for the homeless, exiled, hungry, and forsaken. Catholic Workers continue to protest injustice, war, racism, and violence of all forms." While the majority of Catholic Worker houses are in the United States, there is a small number of residences in Mexico, Canada, Australia, New Zealand, Germany, Great Britain, and the Netherlands.

A Catholic Worker for nearly fifty years

Maurin died in 1949 and Day carried on the leadership of the Catholic Worker movement and newspaper for almost thirty more years. In 1972 Day was presented with the Laetare Medal for outstanding American Catholicism. On giving Day the medal, Notre Dame president Theodore Hesburgh stated, "Dorothy Day has been comforting the afflicted and afflicting the comfortable all her life."

Day gave her last public speech in 1976, after which she suffered a series of heart attacks. Toward the end of her life Day remarked that her ultimate goal had been "to bring about a society where it is easier for men to be good." She died on November 29, 1980, with her daughter at her bedside. Day was buried in the neighborhood in which she had resided for nearly fifty years. Thousands of people—both the powerful and the poor—paid tribute at her funeral.

Sources

Books

Coles, Robert. *Dorothy Day: A Radical Devotion.* Reading, MA: Addison-Wesley Publishing Company, Inc., 1987.

Coles, Robert. *A Spectacle Unto the World: The Catholic Worker Movement.* New York: Viking Press, 1973.

"Day, Dorothy." *American National Biography.* Vol. 6. Edited by John A. Garraty and Mark C. Carnes. New York: Oxford University Press, 1999.

Day, Dorothy. *The Long Loneliness: The Autobiography of Dorothy Day.* New York: Harper & Brothers Publishers, 1952.

Miller, William D. *Dorothy Day: A Biography.* New York: Harper & Row, 1982.

Piehl, Mel. *Breaking Bread: The Catholic Worker and the Origin of Catholic Radicalism in America.* Philadelphia: Temple University Press, 1982.

Articles

Coles, Robert. "Secular Days, Sacred Moments." *America.* January 17, 1998: 4.

"The Gifts of Saint Dorothy Day." *U.S. Catholic.* November 1998: 14.

Whitman, Alden. "Dorothy Day, Outspoken Catholic Activist, Dies at 83." *New York Times.* November 30, 1980.

Web Sites

The Catholic Worker Movement. [Online] Available http://catholicworker. org (accessed December 9, 1999).

Forest, Jim. "A Biography of Dorothy Day." [Online] Available http://www.awadagin.com/cw/ddaybio.htm (accessed December 9, 1999).

Barbara Deming

Born July 23, 1917
New York, New York
Died August 2, 1984
Sugarloaf Key, Florida

Peace and civil rights activist, author, and poet

For more than two decades Barbara Deming was a leader in movements promoting peace, civil rights, women's rights, and lesbian and gay rights. A self-described "radical pacifist lesbian feminist," she challenged others to be true to nonviolence and personal liberties. She also pushed for the acceptance of lesbians within movements for social change and in society at large. In her later years Deming came to view her advocacy for disadvantaged groups as an outgrowth of her own oppression as a lesbian.

Deming wound together the threads of the various movements in which she was involved—peace, antiracism, women's rights, and lesbian and gay rights—into a quest for a more just society.

Quaker and bohemian influences during youth

Deming was born into a wealthy family in New York City on July 23, 1917. She was the second of four children and the only daughter of Katherine Burritt, a singer, and Harold Deming, a noted Republican lawyer. Throughout her youth Deming was surrounded by her mother's eccentric friends from Greenwich Village.

From kindergarten through the twelfth grade Deming attended the Friends School of Fifteenth Street Meeting. The

Barbara Deming.
Reproduced by permission of AP/Wide World Photos.

school, run by Quakers (a religious organization that stresses nonviolence and simple living), gave Deming an early introduction to pacifism—an ideal to which she remained committed throughout her life.

During Deming's teenage years her family owned a country home. Among their neighbors in the countryside were several people with great artistic talent, including poets Edna St. Vincent Millay (1892–1950) and e. e. cummings (1894–1962), photographer Consuelo Kanaga (1894–1978), and painter Annie Poor (1918–), with whom Deming formed a life-long friendship.

Comes to terms with lesbianism

Deming herself was writing poetry by age seventeen. Also at age seventeen Deming had a lesbian relationship with Norma Millay—the sister of Edna St. Vincent Millay. Forty years after that experience Deming wrote the following to her mother about discovering her sexual identity: "I have always been grateful to you for the fact that when you first told me about homosexuality you spoke of it very simply and did not condemn it to me as anything ugly. Because of this, when I fell in love with Norma I felt no hatred of myself."

Deming enrolled in Bennington College in Bennington, Vermont, in 1934. There she studied drawing with the antiestablishment German painter George Grosz (1893–1959). Deming graduated from Bennington with a bachelor's degree in theater in 1938 and two years later completed a master's degree in theater from Western Reserve University (later renamed Case Western Reserve University) in Cleveland, Ohio. Throughout her college years she honed her skills as an essayist, poet, and short-story writer.

Career as a writer

In 1942 Deming was hired as a film analyst for a project of the Library of Congress based at New York's Museum of Modern Art. She also started writing her first book, based on the film analyses she did during the period, titled *Running Away from Myself—A Dream Portrait of America Drawn from the Films of the '40s* (the book was not published until 1969).

Using money given to her by an aunt, Deming traveled through Europe in the early 1950s. While abroad she wrote numerous short stories and began work on an autobiographical novel. The short stories were published in 1974 as *Wash Us and Comb Us*. The novel, titled *A Humming Under My Feet: A Book of Travail,* was published in 1985.

In 1954 Deming met artist Mary Meigs, and the two became companions. They moved to Wellfleet, Massachusetts, where Deming continued her writing career. A small number of Deming's poems, short stories, and essays were published in the *Partisan Review* and *New Yorker* magazines.

Visits India and Cuba

Deming and Meigs traveled to India in 1959—twelve years after India's independence from British rule and eleven years after the assassination of the legendary leader **Mohandas (Mahatma) Gandhi** (1869–1948; see entry). While in India, Deming studied the philosophy of nonviolence taught by Gandhi and deepened her own commitment to pacifism and to challenging society's injustices.

In 1960 Deming traveled to Cuba, where the previous year Fidel Castro's (1927–; see box in "Ché" Guevara entry) revolutionary forces had toppled the U.S.-backed dictator Fulgencio Batista. Deming had the good fortune of a chance meeting with Castro. The Cuban leader discussed with Deming his beliefs that the greedy practices of American corporations had reduced the Cuban people to poverty. Deming toured the small island nation to see for herself the effects of decades of exploitation.

Conversion to an activist

Deming's Cuba trip, like her visit to India, had a profound influence on her thinking and future. She returned to the United States a committed peace activist and became involved in three organizations: the Peacemakers, the Committee for Nonviolent Action (a Gandhian group), and the War Resisters League. She participated in, and was arrested during, some of the earliest protests against nuclear weapons testing.

"Those struggles in which I took part," explained Deming in a 1984 interview with *Ms.* magazine, "the strug-

Gay-Rights Activist
Harry Hay

Harry Hay (1912–)—an organizer, writer, actor, and philosopher—was one of the pioneers of the gay-rights movement in the United States. He began working for gay rights two decades before the Stonewall Rebellion—the 1969 event that most people consider the start of the gay liberation movement in America.

In 1950 Hay and four friends formed the first American organization to advocate for the civil liberties and human rights of gay people: the Mattachine Society. It was a secret organization because members feared that if they were found out they would lose their jobs. As a leader of the Mattachine Society, Hay wrote and spoke extensively on gay rights, organized protests, conferences, and workshops, and established society chapters around the country.

Hay stood up for the rights of gay people during the McCarthy-era 1950s, counseled gay draft resisters in the Vietnam-era 1960s, and argued for creativity and radicalism within the mainstream gay-rights movement in the

Harry Hay. *Photograph by Daniel Nicoletta. Reproduced by permission.*

conservative 1990s. In 1996 Hay published a collection of essays and political speeches titled *Radically Gay: Gay Liberation in the Words of Its Founder.* In his book Hay made the argument that gays are a cultural minority, with a shared history and common values. He also stressed the importance of self-acceptance for gay men and lesbians, and attacked the growing antigay sentiment in the United States.

gle against my countrymen's abuse of blacks, the Cuban people, the Vietnamese—each of these struggles reverberated deeply a so-called apolitical struggle I'd been waging on my own, in a lonely way up until then, as a woman and a lesbian: the struggle to claim my life as my own, to affirm that it didn't belong to the patriarchs, it belonged to *me.* . . . Now I can see that the reason I gave my support with such passion was that I was waging my own fight by analogy. What an amazing feeling it was to be struggling at last not just by myself but in community."

Integrates peace and civil rights issues

In the early 1960s Deming was drawn to the blossoming Civil Rights movement. Deming felt that the struggles for civil rights and peace had much in common, and made it her personal quest to integrate the two movements. To that end, Deming organized a peace walk called the Quebec-Washington-Guantanamo Walk for Peace. The walk left Quebec, Canada, on May 26, 1963, and ended after 2,800 miles in Miami, Florida, on May 29, 1964.

During the course of the walk Deming was arrested in Birmingham, Alabama, and in three Georgia cities: Macon, Griffin, and Albany. In Albany marchers were arrested and jailed for four weeks for refusing to follow the path through town prescribed by the police chief. Deming later wrote a book about her stay in the Albany jail titled *Prison Notes.*

Deming was also an outspoken critic of the Vietnam War (1954–75). In addition to organizing antiwar protests in the United States, Deming traveled to Vietnam and witnessed the American bombing of Hanoi. In 1971 Deming published a book about her experiences during the Vietnam War titled *Revolution and Equilibrium.*

Shifts focus to women's and gay rights

In the 1970s Deming turned her energy towards two issues that affected her personally: women's rights and gay and lesbian rights. In 1971, after many years of keeping her sexual identity secret, Deming "came out" as a lesbian to her friends in the Civil Rights and peace movements.

In 1974 Deming published *We Cannot Live Without Our Lives,* a book about violence against women. Her 1981 publication, *Remembering Who We Are,* addressed the oppression of women in society throughout history. In the mid-1970s Deming and her partner Jane Gapen moved to Sugarloaf Key, Florida, and established a women's community.

Deming brought together her passions for peace and women's rights in 1983, when she participated in the Women's

Encampment for a Future of Peace and Justice. The encampment took place at a women's commune near the Seneca Army Depot (a nuclear missile storage site) in Romulus, New York. The women staged frequent protests at the army depot. In one instance, as the women marched to the army depot, they were confronted by an angry mob of armed men. In response, the women sat down in the road and refused to move. Police moved in and arrested fifty-four women (who became known as the "Waterloo Fifty-four"), among them Deming. The women were detained for five days, after which they were released and the charges dropped.

Diagnosed with cancer

In February 1984 Deming was diagnosed with ovarian cancer, after which she underwent surgery and months of painful chemotherapy and radiation. Shortly before her death Deming returned home from the hospital, where she died on August 2, 1984, surrounded by friends and family members.

"Esteem for Deming continued to grow after her death," wrote Carolynne Myall in *Gay and Lesbian Literature,* "especially among pacifist, feminist, and lesbian activists, for whom she was a model. Since her art and activism were linked, it remained difficult to separate admiration for Deming's living from admiration for her writing."

After Deming's death, a group of her friends compiled some of her old and new writings into a book called *Prisons That Could Not Hold* (1985). That book contains a reprint of Deming's 1966 *Prison Notes,* an account of her jailing in upstate New York in 1983 titled "A New Spirit Moves Among Us," a joint statement by the women in jail with Deming on that occasion, a short biography of Deming, and an interview with Deming by the Boston Women's Video Collective.

Sources

Books

"Barbara Deming." *Gay and Lesbian Biography.* Detroit: St. James Press, 1997.

Deming, Barbara. *Prison Notes.* New York: Grossman Publishers, 1966.

Deming, Barbara. *Prisons That Could Not Hold.* San Francisco: Spinsters Ink, 1985.

Deming, Barbara. *Revolution and Equilibrium.* New York: Grossman Publishers, 1971.

Deming, Barbara, and Jane Meyerding. *We Are All Part of One Another: A Barbara Deming Reader.* Philadelphia: New Society Publishers, 1984.

Deming, Barbara. *We Cannot Live Without Our Lives.* New York: Grossman Publishers, 1974.

McDaniel, Judith. "Barbara Deming." *American National Biography.* Vol. 6. Edited by John A. Garraty and Mark C. Carnes. New York: Oxford University Press, 1999, pp. 416–17.

Articles
"Barbara Deming." (Obituary.) *New York Times.* August 4, 1984: 28.

Fritz, Leah. "We Are All Part of One Another: A Tribute to Barbara Deming." *Ms.* December 1984: 41+.

Marian, Morton J. Review of *Prisons That Could Not Hold. Mississippi Quarterly.* Winter 1996: 229+.

Frederick Douglass

Born 1817
Tuckahoe, Maryland
Died 1895
Washington, D.C.

Escaped slave, abolitionist, orator, and author

"[Slavery's] peaceful annihilation is almost hopeless . . . the slave's right to revolt is perfect. The slaveholder has been tried and sentenced, his execution only waits the finish to the training of his executioners. He is training his own executioners."

Frederick Douglass in his memoirs

Frederick Douglass.
Public Domain

Frederick Douglass escaped from slavery at the age of seventeen to become one of the most effective abolitionists and most celebrated speakers and authors in the United States. He founded the abolitionist weekly newspaper *North Star.* The newspaper's office served as a way station on the Underground Railroad (the secret network through which slaves were assisted to freedom). Even after the emancipation of the slaves Douglass championed equal rights for African Americans and for women.

Born into slavery

Frederick Douglass was born into slavery in Tuckahoe, Maryland, in 1817 (the exact date of his birth was not recorded). He knew his mother—a slave named Harriet Bailey—only briefly, as she was sold to another plantation when he was a baby. (At the time it was common for slaveholders to separate children from their mothers before the child's first birthday.) Douglass never knew the identity of his father; he only knew that his father was a white man. His father was most likely his master, Captain Aaron Anthony.

Douglass lived with his grandparents, Betsey and Isaac Bailey, for his first seven years. They resided in a two-story windowless cabin with a clay floor in the little town of Tuckahoe. The Baileys, also the property of Anthony, were charged with raising the children of plantation slaves so that the children's parents could work in the fields.

Plantation life

When Douglass reached the age of seven, he was forced to move into a house for slaves on the plantation, as was customary for slave children. Too young to labor in the fields, Douglass was responsible for tending the cows and chickens, keeping the barnyard clean, and running errands. Removed from the care of his grandmother, he was placed under the watchful eye of a household slave named Aunt Katy.

Aunt Katy and Douglass did not get along well. Katy had a quick temper and often punished Douglass by hitting or kicking him. Sometimes she withheld his food (which consisted of corn mush set on the ground in a large wooden tray, for the children to fight over). Douglass suffered much more from the cold than from hunger, he wrote later, as he had no shoes, socks, pants, or jacket—only a coarse cloth shirt that hung to his knees. On the coldest nights he slept, head-first, in a burlap corn storage bag on a dirt floor. When Douglass was seven years old he learned that his mother had died.

Adolescence in Baltimore

In 1825, at the age of eight, Douglass was sent to work for his master's relatives, Hugh and Sophia Auld, in Baltimore, Maryland. Douglass's job was to help look after Tommy, the Auld's young son. Douglass was given food, clothing, and a warm bed. Mrs. Auld treated Douglass with kindness. She even included Douglass in Tommy's reading lessons. After two years, when Mr. Auld found out about the lessons, he told his wife that it was against the law to educate a slave and forbade Douglass to read. Douglass did just the opposite. He secretly read everything he could get his hands on.

Douglass lived with the Aulds until 1833, when he was ordered back to the plantation. Douglass was disappointed to leave the Aulds and his friends—black and white—of the bustling port city.

Nat Turner (left) being held at gunpoint.
Courtesy of the Library of Congress.

Stands up to his master

The plantation had a new owner, another Anthony relative named Thomas Auld, who was both greedy and cruel. He worked his slaves to near exhaustion and starvation. When the other slaves found out that Douglass knew how to read they begged him to start a Sunday school for black children. One Sunday morning the lessons were broken up by an angry mob of local white men, including Douglass's master. For punishment Douglass was sent to the farm of Edward Covey. Covey was considered the best slave breaker (one who "tamed" slaves into submission by breaking their spirit) in the state.

After six months of being worked seven days a week, starved, and beaten, Douglass ran away briefly from Covey's farm. When Douglass returned Covey attacked him in the barn. To Covey's surprise, Douglass fought back. After two hours Covey gave up. Douglass did not get whipped again in his remaining six months at Covey's farm. It was Covey, not Douglass, who had been broken.

Freedom bound

On January 1, 1834, Douglass was sent by his master to work at the farm of William Freeland. There Douglass conspired with five other slaves to escape. Somehow their plan was discovered and they were all arrested and put in jail.

Thomas Auld, fed up with his rebellious slave, sent Douglass back to Hugh and Sophia Auld in Baltimore. Hugh Auld found Douglass a job in the shipyards as a caulker (one who applies waterproof material to the seams of ships). On Saturdays Douglass would hand over his week's wages to the Aulds. They would then sometimes return a few pennies to Douglass as an allowance.

Douglass was very unhappy that he had to work all week and then turn over his wages to his master. He also

Nat Turner's Slave Rebellion

In 1831, just three years before Douglass escaped to freedom, slave preacher Nat Turner (1800–1831) led one of the most violent revolts of the American slavery era. On August 22 of that year Turner and six other black men, armed with only axes and hatchets, began their rebellion in Southampton County, Virginia. The group first killed Turner's master and his family. Throughout the day the group, which had increased to seventy slaves, killed sixty whites.

The rebellion was put down by white troops who killed more than 100 blacks, many of whom were not involved in the rebellion. Several members of Turner's group were tortured to death. Turner himself evaded capture for nearly three months, after which he was caught and executed.

The uprising instilled a great fear in southern slaveholders, who realized that if a docile preacher such as Turner was capable of such violent resistance, then every slave was a threat. As a result, white southerners stockpiled weapons and ammunition and placed further restrictions on the activities of their slaves.

resented the fact that he could not live with the woman he loved and wanted to marry, a free African American named Anna Murray. On September 3, 1838, instead of going to work, Douglass went to the house of a friend—a free African American sailor—who agreed to help him escape. With his friend's papers that said he was a free man, and his friend's clothes that made him look like a sailor on shore leave, Douglass boarded a train heading north. When the train reached New York City Douglass got off and for the first time set foot on free ground.

Family life

The first thing Douglass did as a free man was to write to Anna Murray and ask her to join him. Douglass then wandered the streets of New York City for three days and nights, penniless, hungry, and tired. On the fourth day he was taken in by David Ruggles, a free African American who was an abolitionist and conductor (one who ventured into the American South to help slaves escape) on the Underground Railroad.

Douglass stayed in New York just long enough for Anna to join him. Ruggles arranged for a minister to marry them. Then he sent the two to New Bedford, Massachusetts, where Douglass would be safer from the slave catchers who were sure to be sent looking for him.

In New Bedford, Douglass and Anna began a family. In two year's time the couple had a daughter (Rosetta, b. 1839) and a son (Lewis Henry, b. 1840). Douglass worked hard to support his family, doing odd jobs for low wages, but took pride in keeping what he earned.

Joins antislavery movement

During their first year in New Bedford the Douglass family joined the Methodist Church. There they met other free African Americans, and Douglass learned more about the antislavery movement. He took out a subscription to *The Liberator,* an abolitionist newspaper published and edited by William Lloyd Garrison (1805–1879). Douglass greatly admired Garrison, a white man who publicly declared that all slaves should be freed immediately and given full rights as American citizens.

On August 11, 1841, Douglass made his debut as a speaker for the abolitionist cause. On that date, a man who had heard Douglass speak about slavery in New Bedford's Methodist Church urged Douglass to take the speaker's platform at a Massachusetts Antislavery Society convention. Douglass was nervous, but his speech drew a standing ovation from the five hundred people in attendance. Douglass was hired by the Antislavery Society to travel through the northern states speaking against slavery.

Douglass faced great odds on the lecture circuit. As an African American in the "free" north he had to travel and lodge in separate quarters from his white companions. He was sometimes threatened and beaten by antiabolitionists. Douglass was many times accused of being too smart and well-spoken to have ever been a slave.

Author, publisher, and journalist

In May 1845 Douglass published *Narrative of the Life of Frederick Douglass*—a short book about his life through 1841.

The book became so popular that Douglass feared his former master would learn his whereabouts. In August 1845, with his new book in hand, Douglass left for a speaking tour of England, Ireland, and Scotland. He returned to the United States in the spring of 1847 with enough money to buy his freedom and start a newspaper.

In the fall of 1847 Douglass moved his family to Rochester, New York, and began printing *North Star*. The newspaper (named for the star that led fugitive slaves north, toward freedom) primarily featured articles by African American writers about slavery. The *North Star* also ran stories about the plight of poor and homeless people, children who were forced to work in factories, and women seeking the right to vote.

In the first edition of *North Star* Douglass wrote: "We solemnly dedicate the *North Star* to the cause of our long oppressed and plundered fellow countrymen. . . . It shall fearlessly assert your rights, faithfully proclaim your wrongs and earnestly demand for you instant and even-handed justice. Giving no quarter to slavery at the South, it will hold no truce with oppressors at the North. While it shale boldly advocate emancipation for our enslaved brethren, it will omit no opportunity to gain for the nominally free complete enfranchisement."

Douglass's printing shop also served as a place of refuge for runaway slaves. In the fifteen years of *North Star's* publication, some four hundred fugitive slaves passed through the shop's doors on their way to freedom in Canada.

Advances black rights in pre-Civil War years

The 1850s—the decade leading up to the Civil War (1861–65)—was an extremely busy time for Douglass. In addition to writing articles and publishing his newspaper, he gave lectures supporting the abolition of slavery and women's suffrage (the right to vote), often braving hostile white mobs and death threats to do so. Douglass also tried to start an industrial school for black youth and strategized with other abolitionists.

Douglass was careful not to directly call for an armed rebellion by slaves—a stance that would have alienated his white abolitionist supporters. His speeches, however, made clear that he wished to see the end of slavery by any means. In 1849 Douglass spoke before a packed audience in Boston, Massachusetts. "There are three millions of slaves in this land," stated Douglass, "held by the United States Government, under the sanction of the American Constitution." He then stated (as he later recalled in his memoirs) that he "would welcome the news that the slaves had risen and that the sable arms which have been engaged in beautifying and adorning the South were engaged in spreading death and devastation there."

By 1856 Douglass had become convinced that an end to slavery would only come about through violence. "[Slavery's] peaceful annihilation is almost hopeless . . . and . . . the slave's right to revolt is perfect," Douglass wrote in his memoirs. "The slaveholder has been tried and sentenced, his execution only waits the finish to the training of his executioners. He is training his own executioners."

Exile, Civil War, and Reconstruction

Among Douglass's colleagues in the struggle for emancipation was **John Brown** (1800–1859; see entry)—a zealous white abolitionist who tried to bring down the slave system by force of arms. When John Brown's attempt to steal weapons from the federal arsenal at Harper's Ferry, Virginia, failed in October 1859, Douglass fled to Canada for fear of being accused as an accomplice.

Douglass returned to the United States at the outbreak of the Civil War (between the slave states of the South and the free states of the North) in 1861. Once the Emancipation Proclamation went into effect on January 1, 1863, and African Americans were allowed to enlist in the Union army, Douglass vigorously recruited soldiers for Massachusetts's all-black regiments. Two of his own sons were the first to enlist. Douglass provided counsel to President Abraham Lincoln (1809–1865; president 1861–65) during the war. During Reconstruction (the post-Civil War era in which emancipated slaves were granted civil rights and the southern states were reincorporated into the nation) he fought for suffrage and civil rights for freed blacks.

Douglass's final years

The last years of Douglass' life were spent in comfort and honor. He enjoyed three successive government appointments, the last being the U.S. minister to Haiti. In 1884 Douglass married for a second time (his first wife, Anna, died in 1882)—a white woman named Helen Pitts. When criticized for marrying a white woman, Douglass replied that his first wife "was the color of my mother, and the second, the color of my father."

Sources

Books

Bisson, Terry. *Nat Turner: Slave Revolt Leader.* New York: Chelsea House Publishers, 1988.

Davidson, Margaret. *Frederick Douglass Fights for Freedom.* New York: Four Winds Press, 1968.

Douglass, Frederick. *The Narrative of the Life of Frederick Douglass, An American Slave.* Cambridge: Harvard University Press, 1988.

Harding, Vincent. *There Is a River: The Black Struggle for Freedom in America.* New York: Harcourt Brace Jovanovich Publishers, 1981.

Logan, Rayford W., and Michael R. Winston, eds. *Dictionary of American Negro Biography.* New York: W. W. Norton & Co., 1982.

Malone, Dumas, ed. *Dictionary of American Biography.* New York: Charles Scribner's Sons, 1936.

McKissick, Patricia, and Frederick McKissick. *Frederick Douglass: The Black Lion.* Chicago: Children's Press, 1987.

Joseph Dulin

Born August 10, 1935
Evansville, Indiana

Educator, youth advocate, and civil rights activist

"It matters not the stage, it matters not the station, it matters not the race, it matters not the age, it's what you're going to do to improve the quality of life for others that matters."

Joseph Dulin in a 1997 newspaper interview.

Joseph Dulin's long and illustrious career as an educator can be summed up as a quest to help at-risk kids. In Detroit and Ann Arbor, Michigan, the visionary educator transformed embattled institutions into outstanding schools. The secret to his success was to create within the school a family structure, consisting of staff, students, parents, and community members. Dulin assumed the role of the watchful, caring, and firm father figure—encouraging and challenging "his children" to do their best. He has been credited with helping transform hundreds of troubled youths from potential dropouts into academic achievers.

Stands up to segregation during youth

Dulin was born on August 10, 1935, in Evansville, Indiana. He was the third of four children born to Charles and Alberta Dulin. Charles Dulin taught adult education for many years, until forced out by a state law requiring teachers to have four-year degrees. With only two years of college, Charles Dulin took a job in a factory and became a union steward. Alberta Dulin supplemented the family's income by cleaning houses.

Dulin attended a mostly African American, Catholic primary school. When he came of age for high school, he opted to attend the Catholic Mater Dei High. After converting to Catholicism (a requirement for admission to the school), Dulin became the school's first African American student.

During Dulin's youth Evansville, like much of America, was segregated (the legally mandated separation of the races). Dulin discovered the meaning of segregation one day when he went into a restaurant, ordered a hamburger, and sat down to eat. He was unaware that African Americans were not permitted to eat in the restaurant but were expected to take out their food. The police came to investigate; so did Dulin's father, who stood up for his son. The elder Dulin's courage forever served as an inspiration to the younger Dulin.

At the age of thirteen Dulin joined the local branch of the National Association for the Advancement of Colored People (NAACP) and participated in efforts to desegregate the city's movie theater. At his high school he protested minstrel shows (a form of entertainment in which whites paint their faces black and act like buffoons) and other expressions of racism, and years later, while in college, he fought for integration of the all-white municipal swimming pool.

Graduates from all-white college

At Mater Dei, teachers and administrators nurtured Dulin's intellectual development, and a superintendent helped him gain admission to St. Joseph's College. Dulin was the first African American student to attend the Catholic college in Rensselaer, Indiana. There he earned a teaching certificate and a degree in physical education. After graduation Dulin sought a job in youth education, but he found the doors to employment closed to him.

Dulin then relocated to Kansas City, Missouri, and took a job as a recreation supervisor, after which he spent six months on active duty in the Army Reserves. Dulin's next move was to Algonquin, Illinois, where he worked at a camp for children from inner-city Chicago.

Teaches and coaches at Iowa school

After another frustrating job search (several times Dulin was offered positions, only to have the offers revoked when the employers discovered he was African American), in 1958 Dulin accepted a position teaching and coaching the basketball team at the all-white St. Mary's High School in West Point, Iowa. Since he was unable to find housing in the mostly white community, Dulin moved into the church rectory.

Dulin threw himself into his duties. As basketball coach, Dulin solicited community support for the team and organized a seven-day-a-week basketball program for all students. His success as an African American teacher-coach in an all-white town was the subject of a lengthy feature in *Hue* magazine and articles in other national publications.

In 1959 Dulin married a teacher named Bessie Johnson. Together they had four children; the marriage later ended in divorce.

Beginning in 1961 Dulin spent his summers in graduate school, earning a master's degree in school administration from Indiana State University. In 1962 he settled in Fort Madison, Iowa (with an African American population of three hundred) and established and became president of an NAACP chapter (he also served as vice-president of the Iowa state conference of the NAACP). In that capacity Dulin organized freedom marches and demonstrations. In one case he pressured organizers of a pancake breakfast to cancel plans for an appearance by "Aunt Jemima." (Aunt Jemima—the trademark name of a pancake mix—is a caricature of a happy house slave or nanny for the master's children. The stereotype is derived from southern white mythology and does not depict a real African American woman.)

Begins teaching in Detroit schools

Dulin left Iowa in 1964 to accept a teaching position in the Detroit public schools. After his third year of teaching, Dulin was named principal of the district's summer school. Dulin's success with at-risk students came to the attention of administrators of St. Martin DePorres High School—a Catholic school in inner-city Detroit. The administrators offered Dulin the position of principal of DePorres, and Dulin accepted. In the fall of 1967 Dulin became the first African American layperson to head a Catholic school anywhere in the United States.

Dulin began his tenure at DePorres during an explosive time in Detroit. The previous summer, mounting racial tensions had given way to rioting. Forty-three lives were lost during a week of violence beginning July 23; DePorres was located in the heart of the riots. While the DePorres student body had been 80 percent white during the 1966–67 school year, the racial composition of the inner city changed following the riots so that the school was nearly 90 percent African American at the start of the 1967–68 school year.

Upon taking over as principal, Dulin began working to establish a sense of unity and family among the school's staff, students, their families, the church, and the community. Dulin's strategy succeeded, as evidenced by the statistic that 83 percent of DePorres' 1968 graduates went on to college. DePorres became the subject of national media attention.

"Joe Dulin never turned his back on the children of DePorres," wrote former DePorres student-turned-attorney (now U.S. District Judge and president of the Michigan Bar) Victoria A. Roberts in the September 1997 issue of *Michigan Bar Journal*. "If anything, he was the missing father figure for many, a role model for all, a living, breathing formula for success. He was our hero."

Fights to save DePorres

In 1970 Dulin received word that the Detroit Catholic diocese (a geographic area administered by a bishop) planned to eliminate funding and close DePorres and other inner-city schools. Dulin did not let DePorres go down without a fight. He charged the Catholic Church hierarchy with racism for ignoring the needs of its African American members. On behalf of the National Black Lay Catholic Caucus, of which he was president, Dulin wrote in a press release dated December 5, 1970: "The failure of the White Archdiocesan Task Force to concern itself with the needs of Black people is totally unacceptable to the Black Community. Blacks have demonstrated, picketed, protested, prayed, cried and believed in the White racist Church in an unfruitful effort to become full human beings and total members of the Church."

To protest the school closings, Dulin and his supporters held work stoppages and even chained shut two Detroit Catholic churches. But church officials were unmoved. (These protests were not Dulin's first actions against racism in the church; he had previously demonstrated for racial equality at the Vatican embassy in Washington, D.C., and had even led a delegation of African American Catholics to the Vatican in Rome.) Dulin and several parents of DePorres students then took over the chancery (business office of a Catholic diocese) of Detroit and held it for eight days. Ultimately those efforts were successful and funding for the inner-city schools was restored. The two-year struggle, however, had taken a personal toll on Dulin, who in 1972 (at the age of thirty-six) suffered a massive heart attack. Dulin resigned from DePorres at the end of the 1971–72 school year.

Becomes principal of nontraditional Ann Arbor high school

After leaving DePorres, Dulin worked for one year at the Friends School of Detroit and for the next year as a community organizer for the Neighborhood Service Organization. In the latter capacity Dulin won acclaim for establishing "freedom schools" (schools set up for students during the strike) during the forty-three day strike by Detroit public school teachers in 1973.

The success of the freedom schools swept Dulin into his next position—principal of a newly created public high school for troubled youths in Ann Arbor, Michigan. The school that Dulin was hired to run in 1974 was called the "alternative school for disruptive youth." Housed in a dilapidated building outside Ann Arbor city limits, the school was essentially a dumping ground for students—most of them African American—who had been cast out of other Ann Arbor public schools for behavioral problems. Dulin rejected the school's name, preferring to call it the "alternative school for beautiful kids." Within the program's first year, students and staff settled on the name Roberto Clemente Student Development Center (after the Puerto Rican baseball star and humanitarian Roberto Clemente).

In 1976 Dulin entered into his second marriage, with Yvonne Willis—a social worker and university professor from Detroit.

Develops school into nationally renowned institution

Over the past quarter-century Dulin has built the Roberto Clemente Center into a unique and successful alternative education program. Due to Dulin's innovations, the school was transformed from a school of last resort to which "disruptive" students were banished, to a respected institution in which 90 percent of the students enrolled by choice and 90 percent of students graduated. In 1994 the Roberto Clemente Center moved into its newly constructed home: a state-of-the-art, seventeen-classroom facility with a capacity for two hundred students.

Today, a sign in the Roberto Clemente lobby reads, "Welcome to the Clemente Family." That sign is no hollow slogan, for Dulin and his staff take seriously the maintenance of a family atmosphere at the school. Dulin personally greets each student every morning with a handshake. Teachers come to students' homes to hold parent-teacher conferences and to deliver report cards. If a student does not show up for school, a staff member calls or drives to the student's home to find out the reason for the absence or to roust the student out of bed. Parents are required to attend one breakfast meeting each semester. And every week there is a schoolwide rap session, at which staff members deliver praise and criticism, and students talk about school issues, their home lives, or anything else on their minds.

Although Dulin's methods are unconventional and controversial, his results are undeniable. One student set straight by Dulin was Aaron Hill—a young man on the brink of dropping out when he came to Roberto Clemente. "At this time last year, he was on the edge of disaster," stated Hill's mother, Dora Hill, in a 1996 newspaper interview. "Now he wants to learn and do his homework. Joe (Dulin) absolutely made a difference. He was always there for him; he calls him at home. Aaron said Joe is like a father to him."

Honors and awards

Dulin has received numerous honors and awards, including the Sojourner Truth Educational Excellence Award, the Man of the Year Award from the Minority Women Group of Michigan in 1994, and a special tribute from the State of

National African American Parent Involvement Day

In 1996 Dulin underscored the essential role that parents play in their children's education, as well as the need for schools to welcome African American parents, when he founded the annual National African American Parent Involvement Day (NAAPID). Dulin conceived of NAAPID at the October 16, 1995, Million Man March (the gathering in Washington, D.C., of one million African American men for the stated purpose of bettering themselves and their communities). A young speaker at the event had challenged attendees to return to their communities and make a positive contribution; Dulin decided his contribution would be NAAPID.

"Joe Dulin empowered black parents to go into their children's schools, to find out what is going on, to hear what is being taught," wrote Victoria A. Roberts regarding NAAPID in the September 1997 issue of *Michigan Bar Journal*. "He empowered parents to ask questions. He empowered parents to be *the* instruments of change to better their children's education."

The first NAAPID was held on February 12, 1996. Schools in forty states, plus the District of Columbia, Puerto Rico, Quebec, Canada, the Virgin Islands, and Australia participated. NAAPID has grown over the years; in 2000 it was observed at schools in at least forty-four states and a handful of foreign countries.

Michigan Senate and House of Representatives for the National African American Parent Initiative Day (NAAPID) Initiative. He was inducted into the Hall of Fame of the National Alliance of Black School Educators in 1997. In March 2000 Dulin was presented with a lifetime achievement award by Wolverine Human Servies (a social service agency in Michigan).

At the dawn of the twenty-first century, Dulin was involved in numerous community groups. For example, he was serving as president of the board of directors of the African American Academy—a Saturday-morning enrichment program affiliated with the Ann Arbor Public Schools. He was also cochairman of the Ann Arbor Public Schools Black Administrators Association, cochairman of the Ann Arbor Public Schools Achievement Initiative, and vice president of the Washtenaw County Community Mental Health Board.

Sources

Articles

Branam, Judson. "Dulin's Day: National Interest Grows in African-American Parents' Involvement." *Ann Arbor News*. December 12, 1995: B1.

"Catholic School Unit Formed in Inner City." *Detroit News*. December 8, 1970: 22A.

Cobbs, Liz. "Dulin: He Wants to Turn a Dream into Reality for Black Teens." *Ann Arbor News*. January 12, 1997.

Evans, Lilly A. "New Clemente Center Dedicated." *Ann Arbor News*. September 19, 1994.

George, Maryanne. "Principal Names Day for Parent Involvement." *Detroit Free Press*. November 8, 1995.

George, Maryanne. "Principal behind National African-American Parent Involvement Day Has Spent 38 Years Challenging Students, Parents." *Knight-Ridder/Tribune News Service*. February 8, 1996.

Manser, Nancy. "Teachers End Strikes at 2 Catholic Schools." *Detroit News*. March 2, 1971.

Miller, Janet. "Adults Hold Key to Child's Success, Speaker Says." *Ann Arbor News*. February 15, 2000: A1+.

"Million Man March Inspires Educator to Start National African-American Parent Involvement Day." *Metro Herald* (Alexandria, VA). January 12, 1996.

"A Million Parents?" *NEA Today*. February 1997: 14.

Roberts, Victoria. "A Tribute to Greatness." *Michigan Bar Journal*. September 1997: 912–15.

Wilkins, Dave. "Clemente Center: A Battle for Respect." *Ann Arbor News*. April 29, 1991: C1+.

Windsor, Patricia. "Turnabout Is Fair Play at Roberto Clemente." *Ann Arbor News*. December 25, 1994.

Wittenberg, Henri E. "Blacks Plan to Seize 2nd Church." *Detroit News*. December 6, 1970: 1A, 23A.

Other

Dulin, Joe. Interview by author. April 8, 2000.

Nawal El Saadawi

Born October 27, 1931
Kafr Tahla, Egypt

Women's rights advocate, psychiatrist, and author

"Now we know where lies our tragedy. We were born of a special sex, the female sex. We are destined in advance to taste of misery, and to have a part of our body torn away by cold, unfeeling cruel hands."

Nawal El Saadawi in
The Hidden Face of Eve

Nawal El Saadawi.
Photograph by Robert Maass.
Reproduced by permission of
Corbis Corporation.

Nawal El Saadawi, considered the Arab world's leading feminist, has broken the silence on many repressive practices to which Arab women are subjected. Her bold denunciations of the patriarchal (male-dominated) system in Arab and Moslem societies has led to her arrest on more than one occasion. El Saadawi's many books (both fiction and nonfiction) about the status of women in the Arab world have been banned for periods of time in her native Egypt and in other Arab nations. Driven from her homeland by death threats, Saadawi spent the 1990s teaching, writing, and speaking in the United States and Europe.

Childhood and education

El Saadawi was born on October 27, 1931, in the Egyptian village of Kafr Tahla. Her father, El Sayed El Saadawi, was a school administrator, and her mother, Zeinabl Shoukry El Saadawi, was a homemaker. El Saadawi attended public schools and, like her siblings, excelled at her studies.

From an early age, however, El Saadawi was made aware of what it meant to be female. Her father often lamented that she was not a boy, implying that girls were of little value. El Saadawi's social education was provided by her aunts—themselves at the beck and call of their husbands and brothers—who taught her to be docile and to attend to the needs of the males in the household.

Undergoes female rite of passage: genital mutilation

A chapter of El Saadawi's childhood was closed at age six, when she was subjected to genital mutilation—the amputation of the clitoris. This practice, also called female circumcision or clitoridectomy, was routinely imposed on girls throughout the Arab world and northern Africa at that time (while the practice was outlawed in Egypt in the 1970s, it is still widespread in rural villages).

In some genital mutilations, after the clitoris is removed (and sometimes the labia as well), the vagina is sewn shut—allowing just a tiny opening for urination and menstruation. The purpose of the female genital mutilation is to dampen the sexual desire of girls and women and to prove to a prospective husband that a girl is a virgin. (In the Arab world, a woman is expected to be a virgin on her wedding night.)

In El Saadawi's case, she and her sister were taken into the bathroom one night and their genitals were cut without anesthetic. "Now we know what it is," El Saadawi recalled of that night in her 1977 book (translated into English in 1980) *The Hidden Face of Eve.* "Now we know where lies our tragedy. We were born of a special sex, the female sex. We are destined in advance to taste of misery, and to have a part of our body torn away by cold, unfeeling cruel hands."

Start of medical career

After high school El Saadawi enrolled in Cairo University in Egypt. Because of her good grades, she was selected to attend the university's medical school (she had little say in the matter, as the best students are directed into the medical school). El Saadawi completed her medical degree in 1955, specializing in thoracic medicine and psychiatry.

In 1956 El Saadawi began working at the Rural Health Center in Tahla, Egypt. There El Saadawi regularly treated girls suffering uncontrollable bleeding and sometimes death as a result of genital cutting. El Saadawi had numerous female patients with recurring infections or lasting psychological injuries from the mutilation. Those experiences led her to call for an end to genital mutilation—a battle cry she continues to sound. (The World Health Organization in 1995 estimated that more than two million girls are subjected to genital mutilation every year. El Saadawi's own research in the early 1990s found that in Egypt, 98 percent of girls in rural areas and 62 percent of girls from educated families had been forced to undergo genital mutilation.)

Becomes director of health education

In 1958 El Saadawi returned to Cairo, Egypt's capital, to accept a post as director of health education at the Ministry of Health. She retained that position until 1972, taking time off to earn a master's degree from Columbia University in New York City in public health (completed in 1966). El Saadawi also served as editor-in-chief of *Health* magazine from 1968 through 1972.

El Saadawi was twice married in the 1950s. Both marriages failed after a year or two due to El Saadawi's husbands' inability to accept her political and professional activities. (Her second marriage, to a lawyer, ended when the man forced El Saadawi to choose between him and her writing career; she chose her writing.) El Saadawi had two children; one from each of the first two marriages.

In 1964 she married fellow activist Sherif Hetata, a writer and physician. In Hetata El Saadawi found a soul mate. Their marriage has lasted more than three decades. Hetata has translated many of El Saadawi's books into English, and the couple teaches and lectures together.

Fired from government post for writings on sexuality

In 1971 El Saadawi published *Women and Sex*—a frank discussion of women's sexuality. In the book El Saadawi not only argued that genital mutilation should be stopped, but said that women have a right to enjoy sex (a truly revolutionary statement in her conservative society). Shortly thereafter, she was fired from her position in the ministry of health and removed as editor of *Health* magazine.

El Saadawi worked as a writer with the High Institute of Literature and Science in Cairo from 1973 through 1978. Her next position, as director of the African Training and Research Center for Women—an agency of the United Nations Economic Commission for Africa—took her to Addis Ababa, Ethiopia, through 1980.

Imprisoned by Anwar Sadat

In 1981 El Saadawi spent nearly three months in prison for her views. She was one of many intellectuals and free-thinkers to be imprisoned by Egyptian President Anwar Sadat (1918–1981) during his rule (1970–1981). The three issues that El Saadawi believe got her into trouble were her advocacy of women's rights, her opposition to the 1979 peace treaty between Egypt and Israel, and her criticism of the Egyptian government for catering to wealthy individuals and foreign nations while ignoring the needs of the impoverished majority of citizens. Her "crime" was officially defined as a violation of her country's "Law for the Protection of Values from Shame."

El Saadawi's arrest, on September 6, 1981, drew protest from women's organizations around the world. On November 25, 1981, following the assassination of Sadat, El Saadawi was released.

"The authorities claimed that I was instigating women toward absolute sexual freedom and immorality," El Saadawi wrote in an essay for the *Contemporary Authors Autobiography* series, "even though in everything I wrote I tried to combat reducing women to being sex objects fit only for seduction and consumption. I was even opposed to women wearing makeup. I encouraged them to be intelligent human beings and not mere bodies to satisfy men, to produce children, or to be slaves."

Prison is an experience El Saadawi shares with her husband. Hetata spent thirteen years in prison for his opposition to government policies before the two married. "Imprisonment in my country," writes El Saadawi, "is always possible for any person who thinks and writes freely. Most of the men and women I know have been in prison some time in their life."

El Saadawi chronicled her time in prison in her *Memoirs from the Women's Prison*, published in 1983 and translated into English in 1986.

El Saadawi's Literary Accomplishments

El Saadawi began writing while a teenager. She now has to her credit eight books of nonfiction, ten novels, seven short story collections, two plays, and scores of essays. Her books, written in Arabic, have been translated into many languages, including English, Danish, Dutch, Finnish, French, German, Italian, Japanese, Norwegian, Portuguese, Swedish, and others. Although El Saadawi's works have been banned throughout much of the Arab world, many copies have made their way into the hands of Arab women. She has won numerous international awards for her books.

El Saadawi's classic work of nonfiction, and her first writing to be translated into English, is *The Hidden Face of Eve: Women in the Arab World* (1977; English translation in 1980). This book brought the plight of Arab women to the attention of the Western world. In it El Saadawi describes the physical and mental abuses to which some Arab women and girls are subjected, including genital mutilation, wife-beating, polygamy (men taking more than one wife), and arranged marriages of girls to older men.

Similarly, El Saadawi explores the oppression of women under Arab governments and Islamic religion in her novels. One of her earliest novels, *Woman at Point Zero,* (1975; English translation in 1983), tells the story of a woman forced

Founds Arab Women's Solidarity Association

In 1982 El Saadawi founded the Arab Women's Solidarity Association (AWSA), an international group of Arab women committed to "lifting the veil from the mind" of women. The AWSA was granted consultative status as a nongovernmental organization of the United Nations in 1985. Among its primary functions, the AWSA organized conferences and weekly discussions on the status of women in the Arab world.

The Egyptian government, in June 1991, shut down the AWSA and its magazine. The move was interpreted as a censure for Saadawi's opposition to the Gulf War (1991)—particularly her denunciation of the United States's role in the conflict (she felt the Iraq-Kuwait problem should be solved by Arab nations). The Egyptian government transferred all funds to work as a prostitute in order to survive in a man's world. In her next novel, *God Dies by the Nile* (1976; English translation in 1985), she writes about corrupt politicians and their reign of terror over women and poor people. *The Circling Song* (1977; English translation in 1989) is set in a land where women undergo rape and genital mutilation as a rite of passage. *The Fall of the Imam* (1987; English translation in 1988) addresses the hypocrisy of a culture in which it is acceptable for men to be sexually promiscuous while women are expected to be chaste. *The Innocence of the Devil* (1992; English translation in 1994), in which God and the devil are both patients in an insane asylum, is a study of the influence of religion on the social role of women.

El Saadawi insists that the experiences of women in her novels are not unique to Arab or Moslem societies. "The oppression of women . . . constitutes an integral part of the political, economic, and cultural system preponderant in most of the world," stated El Saadawi in an interview. "It is born of developments in history that made one class rule over another and men dominate over women."

In 1999 El Saadawi published a remembrance of her early years, titled *A Daughter of Isis: The Autobiography of Nawal El Saadawi.*

from AWSA to a religious women's group. El Saadawi went to court seeking relief from the order, but the government's position was upheld.

Driven into exile by death threats

Even after her release from prison, El Saadawi was banned from appearing on Egyptian radio and television. Her continuing criticisms of Islamic leadership and religious practices that subjugate women earned her a place on a list of twenty writers targeted for death by Islamic fundamentalists. The government was forced to provide El Saadawi with round-the-clock armed bodyguards.

In 1992, following the killing of a close associate—Egyptian intellectual Faraj Fuda—by Islamic extremists, El Saadawi chose to leave Egypt. She accepted a position on the faculty of Duke University in Durham, North Carolina, remaining there until 1996 (she spent six months in 1994 as a visiting professor at the University of Washington in Seattle).

As the 1990s came to a close, El Saadawi continued to travel widely throughout North America and Europe, speaking out for women's rights and for the end of wealthy nations' domination over poor nations. "You cannot separate the liberation of women from the liberation of the land and the economy and the culture and the language," stated El Saadawi in a 1994 interview.

Sources

Books

El Saadawi, Nawal. *A Daughter of Isis: The Autobiography of Nawal El Saadawi*. Translated by Sherif Hetata. London, England: Zed Books, 1999.

El Saadawi, Nawal. *God Dies by the Nile*. Translated by Sherif Hetata. London, England: Zed Books, 1985.

El Saadawi, Nawal. *The Hidden Face of Eve: Women in the Arab World*. Translated by Sherif Hetata. Boston: Beacon Press, 1980.

El Saadawi, Nawal. *The Innocence of the Devil*. Berkeley: University of California Press, 1994.

El Saadawi, Nawal. *Memoirs from the Women's Prison*. Translated by Marilyn Booth. Berkeley: University of California Press, 1986.

Malti-Douglas, Fedwa. *Men, Women, and God(s): Nawal El Saadawi and Arab Feminist Poetics*. Berkeley: University of California Press, 1995.

Articles

Jacoby, Susan. "Nawal El Saadawi: A Woman Who Broke the Silence." *Washington Post*. November 27, 1994: X3.

Katz, Alyssa. "Portrait of the Activist as a Young Girl." *Village Voice*. September 14, 1999: 66.

Lancaster, Pat. "Unveiling the Mind." *Middle East*. December 1997: 40+.

Lieblich, Julia, and Delia M. Rios. "Perilous Passage: Despite Opposition, Ritual Circumcisions Threaten the Physical and Emotional Health of More than 2 Million Young Women a Year." *The Times-Picayune* (Newhouse News Service). September 6, 1995: E1.

Winokur, Julie. "Uncensored: Egypt's Most Outspoken Feminist Sets Up Her Soapbox at the UW." *Seattle Times*. April 24, 1994: 12.

Frantz Fanon

Born July 20, 1925
Martinique, French Antilles
Died December 6, 1961
Bethesda, Maryland

Psychiatrist, philosopher, political revolutionary, and author

Frantz Fanon (pronounced Fah-NAWN) grew up in the French-colonized island of Martinique. (Colonialism is the policy by which one nation exerts control over another nation or territory.) After serving in World War II (1939–45), he studied medicine in France. As a psychiatrist, Fanon analyzed the impact of racism and colonialism on colonized people—topics with which he was well familiar.

While working in a government hospital in the French colony of Algeria, in Africa, Fanon became involved with the Algerian independence movement. He came to the conclusion that the only salvation of colonized people was to overthrow their colonizers in violent revolutions. As Fanon explained in his book *The Wretched of the Earth,* a new, just society would rise from the ashes of the old one. Fanon's philosophy was eagerly embraced by Africans and African Americans—people who were victims of colonialism and racism and were hungry for liberation.

Early lessons in racism

Fanon was born on July 20, 1925, to middle-class parents on the French-protectorate island of Martinique. (Mar-

Fanon was a founding father of the Algerian struggle for liberation from French rule. His writings provided the philosophical underpinnings for subsequent movements against racism and colonialism around the world.

tinique is part of the French Antilles—the chain of islands in the Caribbean stretching from Puerto Rico to the northeastern tip of Venezuela.) Fanon was the descendent of slaves brought to the Antilles from Africa. His father worked as a customs inspector.

As a young student in the French-run public school system, Fanon was taught French language and culture. He was looked down upon by his white schoolteachers because of his black skin.

Fights with French forces in World War II

Fanon was drafted to serve in the French army during World War II. In 1944 he fought with the Free French forces (the forces opposing the Nazis—an abbreviation for the Nationalist Socialist German Worker's Party, an authoritarian and anti-Semitic political party headed by Adolf Hitler) in northern Africa and Europe. He was wounded in action near the Swiss border, after which he was given a medal for bravery and discharged.

In the military Fanon experienced rampant racism on two levels: soldiers from the colonies (such as himself) were discriminated against by white troops, and native Africans were discriminated against by white European settlers.

Pursues career in medicine

At the end of the war Fanon briefly returned to Martinique. There he supported the successful campaign of Communist candidate Aimé Césaire to the National Assembly. In 1946 Fanon received a scholarship and enrolled in medical school in Lyons, France (he was one of five of the eight children in his family to attend a French university). In addition to taking science classes, Fanon studied the writings of Friedrich Nietzsche (German philosopher, 1844–1900), **Karl Marx** (German economist and philosopher, 1818–1883; see entry), and Jean-Paul Sartre (French philosopher, 1905–1980)—all three of whom offered critiques of materialism and capitalist society.

Toward the end of his schooling, Fanon did a case study of a population of North African immigrants living in France. He graduated with a medical degree, in 1950, with a specialty in psychiatry. In 1952 he married a French woman named Marie-Josephe (Josie) Duble. The couple had one son, named Oliver.

Practices psychiatry in Blida, Algeria

From November 1953 through January 1957 Fanon served as head of the psychiatric department at a government hospital in the city of Blida (the most important psychiatric hospital in Africa), in the French colony of Algeria. Based on his experiences with racism, he took an unconventional approach to dealing with the mental disorders of Algerians. Rather than regarding black Algerians' disorders as arising from solely within those individuals, he looked at the impacts of racism and colonialism on his patients. He concluded that the only way to heal individuals was to change society.

Fanon prepared to resign from his psychiatric position in 1956. "Madness is one of the means man has of losing his freedom," he wrote in his resignation letter. "And I can say, on the basis of what I have been able to observe from this point of vantage, that the degree of alienation of the inhabitants of this country is frightening. If psychiatry is the medical technique that aims to enable man no longer to be a stranger to his environment, I owe it to myself to affirm that the Arab, permanently an alien in his own country, lives in a state of absolute depersonalization."

Writes on racism and colonialism

Fanon wrote four books during his brief life about the psychological and material consequences of racism and colonialism. In his first book, *Black Skin, White Masks* (1952), he explained that one effect of colonialism was to rob indigenous people of their own history and culture. White colonizers, moreover, made black and brown people feel ashamed of the color of their skin. He argued that black people in a white-dominated world were made to try to hide their blackness under a "white mask." Colonized people, he concluded, were made to hate everything about themselves and their culture and to love their colonizers and emulate the colonizers' culture.

Fanon compiled two collections of essays—*Studies in a Dying Colonialism* (1959) and *Toward the African Revolution* (published posthumously in 1964)—which told of his thoughts on racism and colonialism from the time he began practicing psychiatry in Algeria until his death. He advocated the formation of a unified Africa, free from racial and cultural prejudices. Fanon's final book was *The Wretched of the Earth* (1961). Written by Fanon on his deathbed, the book inspired revolutionary struggles around the world (see box).

Joins Algerian nationalist movement

During Fanon's second year in Algeria, armed rebellion broke out in Blida. Fanon came into contact with Algerians working for their nation's independence and quietly supported them for three years. He hid rebels in his hospital, trained nurses for the underground movement, relayed sensitive information, and offered space for secret meetings. He even taught combatants how to psychologically endure torture at the hands of their enemies.

Fanon's role in the Algerian independence movement was discovered in late 1956, and he was ordered to leave the country. Fanon then moved to neighboring Tunisia (a country recently granted its independence from France) and secured a position at the Manouba Clinic and Neuropsychiatric Center in the capital city of Tunis. Fanon also taught classes at the University of Tunis.

In the relative safety of Tunisia, Fanon openly worked with the Algerian revolutionary movement. He wrote articles for two rebel newspapers: *El Moudjahid,* of the National Liberation Front, and *Resistance Algerienne,* of the National Liberation Army. Fanon became one of the liberation movement's leading political theorists and spokespersons.

Fanon also brought the message of Algerian independence to international audiences. He went to Paris for the First Congress of Black Writers and Artists in 1956, and attended the All African People's Conference in Accra, Ghana, in 1958. (Ghana obtained its independence from Great Britain in 1957.) In 1960 Fanon served as ambassador to Ghana for the Algerian Provisional Government—the ruling body of the Algerian revolutionary forces.

The Wretched of the Earth Conveys Shocking Message

Fanon's *The Wretched of the Earth*, published in 1961, was his consummate work. Fanon's analysis of his observations of colonial society concluded with a prescription for healing the wounds of colonized people: violent overthrow of the oppressors. Fanon believed that a social revolution must be led by and carried out by the impoverished masses of people (the "wretched of the earth")—not by intellectuals, foreigners, or professional soldiers. Only impoverished people had not been corrupted by materialism, he argued, and therefore only they would be capable of producing an economically and socially just society.

Fanon's most controversial point was his assertion that a racist, colonial system could—and should—only be brought down by violent means. "At the level of individuals," wrote Fanon, "violence is a cleansing force. It frees the native from his inferiority complex and from his despair and inaction; it makes him fearless and restores his self-respect."

The Wretched of the Earth quickly became an international classic. It inspired independence fighters in colonized nations throughout Africa, as well as black nationalists in the United States.

Falls ill with leukemia

In 1961 Fanon became ill and was diagnosed with leukemia (cancer of the blood). He first went to the Soviet Union for treatment. After showing no improvement, he flew to the United States for further treatment at the National Institutes for Health in Bethesda, Maryland. By the time Fanon arrived in the United States, however, it was too late. The disease had progressed to the point that it was incurable. Fanon spent his final months completing *The Wretched of the Earth*.

One month before his death, Fanon wrote the following to his friend Roger Tayeb: "Death is always with us and . . . what matters is not to know whether we can escape it but whether we have achieved the maximum for the ideas we have made our own. . . . We are nothing on this earth if we are not in the first place the slaves of a cause, the cause of the peoples, the cause of justice and liberty. I want you to know that even when the doctors had given me up, in the gathering dusk I was still thinking of the Algerian people, of the peoples of the Third World, and when I have persevered, it was for their sake."

Fanon died on December 6, 1961, just one week after receiving the first copy of his book *The Wretched of the Earth.* He did not live to see Algerian independence from France, which was achieved on July 5, 1962. Fanon's body, in accordance with his stated wishes, was flown back to Tunisia. From there it was transported by Algerian nationalists to rebel-held territory in Algeria for burial.

Sources

Books
Fanon, Frantz. *Black Skin, White Masks.* Boston: Grove Press, 1967.

Fanon, Frantz. *The Wretched of the Earth.* Boston: Grove Press, 1965.

"Frantz Fanon." *Encyclopedia of World Biography.* Farmington Hills, MI: The Gale Group, 1998.

Gendzier, Irene L. *Frantz Fanon: A Critical Study.* New York: Pantheon Books, 1973.

Zahar, Renate. *Frantz Fanon: Colonialism and Alienation.* Translated by Willfried F. Feuser. New York: Monthly Review Press, 1974.

Articles
Hussein, Adam M. "Frantz Fanon as a Democratic Theorist." *African Affairs.* October 1993: 499+.

Paulo Freire

Born 1921
Recife, Brazil
Died May 2, 1997
Sao Paulo, Brazil

**Educator, literacy advocate,
social reformer, and author**

Freire viewed literacy as a tool for the liberation and self-affirmation of victims of oppression.

Paulo Freire believed that the world's oppressed millions of illiterate adults had a right to an education. He asserted that literacy programs should be developed by students and teachers together and not imposed on the students by privileged outsiders. Freire's method of teaching adults to read was based on each student's particular needs. He used words and concepts significant to the lives of his students and incorporated dialogue and problem-solving in his methods.

Through the educational process students (typically peasants or poor workers) learned about their place in the world. They gained the skills they needed to critically assess the social policies and practices responsible for the social order. At the same time, they learned how to challenge the status quo. It was Freire's belief that education was the key to freedom from oppression, as well as reaching one's full human potential. Many of the social movements of the 1970s, in the United States and elsewhere, were influenced by Freire's philosophy of education for political empowerment.

Paulo Freire.
Reproduced by permission of the Gamma Liaison Network.

Grows up during lean times

Freire was born in 1921 in Recife, in northeastern Brazil. During his youth Brazil experienced an economic depression linked to the Great Depression in the United States (1929–39). Thus, despite his family's middle-class standing (his father was a businessman), Freire and his siblings rarely had enough to eat. Freire experienced hunger pangs and listlessness in school. He vowed to devote his life to the alleviation of hunger, so that other children would not have to suffer.

Conditions improved for the family during Freire's high-school years. After high school graduation Freire enrolled in the Recife University. There he trained to be a teacher, specializing in the planning and implementation of literacy programs. In 1944 Freire married one of his classmates, Elza.

Learns the language of the poor

Freire and his wife both worked as teachers and volunteered with a social service agency, the Catholic Action Movement (CAM). They lived a middle-class lifestyle, as did most of their friends. After a time, the couple became dismayed by the arrogance displayed by their friends and people in the CAM toward people in lower social classes. The Freires were scoffed at for suggesting that their friends' servants should be treated with dignity. The couple ultimately decided to work only with "the people"—Brazil's impoverished majority.

In 1959 Freire completed his doctoral dissertation on the complexities of teaching reading to poor people at Recife University. He explained the necessity of communicating with the poor using words and concepts within their realm of consciousness. The language and experiences of the middle class, he explained, were completely foreign to peasants and workers. Upon earning his Ph.D., Freire became a professor of history and philosophy of education at Recife University.

Heads adult literacy program

In 1962 the mayor of Recife appointed Freire head of the city's adult literacy program. Freire accomplished the astonishing feat of teaching three hundred people to read in just forty-five days. His program continued to demonstrate success, and in 1963 Freire was picked by the president of Brazil to head

The Educational Philosophy of Paulo Freire

Freire viewed society as a struggle between the oppressors and the oppressed, the haves and the have-nots, and the powerful and the powerless. He sided with the oppressed, viewing education as a tool for their empowerment. Freire believed that the educational process should instill in people a critical consciousness, and that such a consciousness would inspire people to transform society. Freire regarded every participant in the classroom as both a teacher and a student, believing that students could all learn from each other's experiences.

In teaching illiterate adults to read and write, Freire started with words from those adults' everyday lives—words that expressed longings, hopes, and frustrations. He then broke those words down into syllables, teaching the students to recognize those syllables in their written form. Freire next recombined the syllables into new words. Using that method, Freire made rapid progress. His students were often able to write short letters to each other after just a few days. While teaching his students to read and write the words, Freire discussed the words' meanings within a larger social context.

Freire was an outspoken critic of educational models that relied on student's memorization of facts. These methods, argued Freire, failed to teach the critical-thinking skills necessary for a students' full participation in society. Freire accused proponents of rote-memorization learning (which he called "banking education") of turning students into unquestioning pawns in economic and political systems that benefit wealthy and powerful minorities. As Freire wrote in *Pedagogy of the Oppressed,* the "banking" style of teaching turns students into "'receptacles' to be 'filled' by the teacher." He continued, "The more completely he fills the receptacles, the better a teacher he is. The more meekly the receptacles permit themselves to be filled, the better students they are."

the National Literacy Program. By 1964 Freire's agency was expected to enroll more than two million students. Freire's literacy techniques were being copied throughout Latin America.

Freire's success, however, threatened the forces intent on upholding the economic and political disparity in Brazil. In 1964, following a military coup (overthrow) that replaced Brazil's president with an army general, Freire's program came under fire. Since literacy was a requirement for voting, it was reasoned, the process of teaching poor people to read and

Myles Horton: Freirian Educator from Tennessee

Myles Horton (1905–1990) was an American educator and activist who, like Freire (his friend and colleague), believed that every individual possessed the power to improve his or her own conditions and make the world a better place for everyone. He also believed that experiential, student-led learning was the key to unlocking every individual's true potential.

Horton put his beliefs into practice at the **Highlander School** (later renamed the Highlander Research and Education Center; see entry) in Tennessee, which he founded and directed for nearly sixty years. The Highlander School offered workshops on labor history, economics, workers' rights, race relations, and organizing strategies. The sessions were informal and directed by the students. That type of education, what Horton termed "experiential learning," was intended to give students the practical skills they needed to deal with real-life situations.

In the 1950s Highlander switched its focus from labor education to civil rights and race relations—in particular the desegregation of public schools in the American South. Because Highlander was an integrated institution in defiance of Jim Crow laws (which called for the separation of the races), it constantly came under fire from racist groups and conservative lawmakers. The Internal Revenue Service, in write would also give those people a voice in the political process. Freire was arrested and jailed for seventy days. He was then ordered to leave the country; it would be sixteen years until he was allowed to return to his homeland.

Teaches and writes while in exile

Freire spent his first five years in exile in Chile. There he was hired by the Chilean Agrarian Reform Corporation to work on a nationwide program for reducing illiteracy. Also during that time he conducted research and wrote three books.

Freire's most famous book is *Pedagogy of the Oppressed* (1970). (Pedagogy is the art or science of teaching.) That book outlined a method of teaching illiterate adults that encourages their participation in the transformation of their societies. It

Myles Horton: Highlander Research and Education Center founder. *Reproduced by permission of AP/Wide World Photos.*

1957, withdrew Highlander's tax-exempt status, and in 1960 the Tennessee courts ordered Highlander to close its doors. Horton left Monteagle, Tennessee, and soon thereafter re-opened the school in Knoxville, Tennessee, renaming it the Highlander Research and Education Center.

Throughout his life Horton remained true to a credo he expressed in his autobiography: "I think that people aren't fully free until they're in a struggle for justice," wrote Horton. "And that means for everyone. It's a struggle of such importance that they are willing, if necessary, to die for it. I think that's what you have to do before you're really free. Then you've got something to live for."

stated that teachers and students must confront sexism and racism as part of the learning process, and that teachers must make students believe in the possibility of social change. *Pedagogy of the Oppressed* was translated into several languages (Freire wrote in his native Portuguese).

Freire moved to the United States in 1969 to accept a teaching position at Harvard University in Cambridge, Massachusetts. His early books, translated into English, had gained him quite a following in the United States.

Works as consultant for World Council of Churches

In 1974 Freire moved to Geneva, Switzerland, to work with the World Council of Churches. He served as a consultant in the Council's office of education, designing literacy programs for various Third World (a term used to describe under-developed countries as a group) countries. Freire's programs met with success in Nicaragua, Chile, Guinea-Bissau, Sudan, and several other countries in Africa.

In the 1970s and 1980s Freire wrote several books on education, politics, and literacy, a sampling of which includes *Education for Critical Consciousness* (1973), *Pedagogy in Process: The Letters to Guinea-Bissau* (1977), *Christian Ideology and Adult Education in Latin America* (1982), *Learning to Question: A Pedagogy of Liberation* (1985), and *Literacy: Reading the Word and the World* (1987).

Final years in Brazil

In 1979 Freire's exile order was lifted and he was allowed to return to Brazil. In 1981 he was hired as a professor of education at the Catholic University of Sao Paulo (Brazil's capital city). In 1991 Freire was made secretary of education for Sao Paulo. He also continued his consultancy with the Institute of Research and Training in Agrarian Reform of the United Nations Educational, Scientific, and Cultural Organization (UNESCO).

Freire died of a heart attack on May 2, 1997, in Sao Paulo. His death came just one year after his 1996 publication *Letters to Cristina*—a series of letters written to his niece Cristina during his years in exile in which he discussed his journey from childhood to adulthood and the educational concerns that comprised his life's work. Throughout his life Freire wrote twenty-five books, which were translated into thirty-five languages. His final works, *Teachers as Cultural Workers: Letters to Those Who Dare Teach* and *Pedagogy of Freedom: Ethics, Democracy, and Civic Courage*, were both published posthumously in 1998.

In an obituary in the *UNESCO Courier*, Freire's friend Frederico Mayor wrote, "Paulo Freire has left us, and with his passing something has gone from the world's classrooms; on every continent teachers have felt, perhaps unconsciously, a moment's sadness before returning to their task with renewed force and conviction."

Sources

Books

Button, John. *The Radicalism Handbook: A Complete Guide to the Radical Movement in the Twentieth Century.* London, England: Cassell, 1995, pp. 158–59.

Freire, Paulo. *Education for Critical Consciousness.* New York: Seabury Press, 1973.

Freire, Paulo. *Letters to Cristina: Reflections on My Life and Work.* Translated by Donalda Macedo, Quilda Macedo, and Alexandre Oliveira. New York: Routledge, 1996.

Freire, Paulo. *Pedagogy of the Oppressed.* Translated by Myra Bergman Ramos. New York: Continuum Publishing, 1970.

Freire, Paulo. *The Politics of Education: Culture, Power, and Liberation.* Translated by Donaldo Macedo. South Hadley, MA: Bergin & Garvey Publishers, Inc., 1985.

Freire, Paulo. *Teachers as Cultural Workers: Letters to Those Who Dare Teach.* Translated by Donaldo Macedo, Dale Koike, and Alexandre Oliveira. Boulder, CO: Westview Press, 1998.

Horton, Myles, with Judith Kohl and Herbert Kohl. *The Long Haul: An Autobiography.* New York: Doubleday, 1990.

"Paulo Freire." *Encyclopedia of World Biography.* Farmington Hills, MI: The Gale Group, 1998.

Articles

D'Olne Campos, Marcio. "Reading the World." *UNESCO Courier.* December 1990: 4+. Interview with Paulo Freire.

Forman, Jack. A review of *Pedagogy of Freedom: Ethics, Democracy, and Civic Courage. Library Journal.* January 1999: 118.

Frederico, Mayor. "Paulo Freire." (Obituary.) *UNESCO Courier.* June 1997: 51.

Review of *Letters to Cristina: Reflections on My Life and Work. Publishers Weekly.* July 22, 1996: 233.

Elizabeth Fry

Born May 21, 1780
Norwich, Norfolk, England
Died October 12, 1845
Ramsgate, Kent, England

English Quaker minister, prison reformer, and advocate for the mentally ill and the homeless

As an advocate for prisoners, the homeless, and the mentally ill, Fry introduced significant reform initiatives in England.

Elizabeth Fry.
Courtesy of the Library of Congress.

Elizabeth Fry worked to improve living conditions for women prisoners, poor people, and the mentally ill. Rooted in the Quaker tradition (Quakers are members of a religious organization that stresses simple living and nonviolence) of performing acts of compassion and charity, Fry provided clothing and education for destitute children and adults, protested harsh prison sentences, founded a homeless shelter in London, England, and helped the unemployed find work. Fry attained a legendary status due to her ceaseless devotion to a population considered dangerous and hopeless by politicians and the public alike.

"For Elizabeth Fry incarceration without an accompanying belief in the ability of the offender to change for the better and to live a meaningful life in the community was unthinkable," wrote George M. Anderson in the October 14, 1995, edition of *America* (150 years after Fry's death). "But she knew that change could begin only when accused persons began to be treated as human beings."

Born into Quaker family

Fry was born in Norwich, in the county of Norfolk (northeast of London), England, on May 21, 1780. She was the third daughter of John Gurney, a successful banker and merchant, and Catherine Gurney, a homemaker. The Gurneys had twelve children in all. Catherine Gurney died in 1792, when Fry was just twelve years old.

The Gurneys belonged to a long line of Quakers. Fry's parents, like many Quakers of their generation, loosened up the strict codes insisted upon by their ancestors. Whereas their forebears had maintained humble surroundings and had associated only with Quakers, the Gurneys accumulated wealth and mingled freely with non-Quakers.

As Fry grew up, her religious convictions became stronger. She resisted her family's drift away from traditional Quakerism. At age eighteen, after listening to a talk by the famous American Quaker preacher William Savery, Fry embraced a more devout and conservative form of Quakerism. She discarded her expensive clothes and adopted the modest Quaker uniform of a simple dress, cap, and hood—attire she donned for the rest of her life. Fry developed a powerful religious sensibility. From time to time she would be overtaken by feelings of religious devotion, stopping whatever she was doing to pray.

Marries and becomes a Quaker minister

In 1800 Fry married Joseph Fry, a London merchant from a strict Quaker background. Over the next sixteen years Fry had ten children (one died in infancy), and bore an eleventh in 1822. In 1811 Fry could no longer stave off what she believed was her true calling and was officially recognized as a Quaker minister. "She spoke with marvelous effect," states the essay about Fry in *The Dictionary of National Biography.* "The pathos of her voice was almost miraculous, and melted alike the hardest criminals and the most impervious men of the world."

Witnesses conditions at Newgate Jail

Fry had first become interested in prison issues at the age of fifteen. At the time she had begged her father to let her visit the corrections house at Norwich, England. Twenty-one

Joyce Dixson: A Modern-Day Advocate for Prisoners' children

Despite the efforts of Elizabeth Fry and other nineteenth-century prison reformers, injustice toward incarcerated individuals and their families remains a problem in the twenty-first century. One modern-day reformer, herself a former prisoner and now an advocate for the children of prisoners, is Joyce Dixson (1951–). Dixson spent seventeen years, from 1976 through 1993, in prison for killing her abusive partner. She earned a bachelor's degree while behind bars and upon her release earned a master's degree in social work from the University of Michigan.

In 1995 Dixson fulfilled her long-term ambition of assisting the children of prisoners when she founded the nonprofit agency Sons and Daughters of the Incarcerated (SADOI). Through SADOI, Dixson gives emotional support to children who are experiencing trauma brought about by the loss of a parent to incarceration. Dixson and social workers under her direction facilitate group sessions in which kids discuss the events that took

years later, married and with a growing brood of children, Fry turned her attention to the plight of female prisoners at the Newgate Jail (in London).

At Newgate Fry found that nearly three hundred women and their children were crowded together in one ward, measuring approximately 190 square yards. They were watched over by two male guards. The inmates washed, cooked, ate, and slept in the same quarters. Placed together were women who had been found guilty of violent crimes, as well as those convicted of minor property offenses and those awaiting trial. The prisoners and their children lacked sufficient clothing and were forced to sleep on the bare floor. There were no rehabilitation programs for the prisoners.

Initiates reforms at Newgate

Fry's first project in the prison was to supply the neediest prisoners with clothes. She then established a school for the prisoners' children. The school was located in an unused

Joyce Dixson (standing). *Reproduced by permission of Joyce Dixson.*

place before, during, and after their parent's incarceration. Dixson recognizes that children of the incarcerated are at a greater risk than the general youth population of becoming criminal offenders; accordingly, one of her goals is to steer her clients away from crime.

Dixson also advocates for reforms in women's prisons, such as disallowing male guards, instituting programs that would allow inmates more contact with their children, and providing greater educational opportunities for inmates.

cell (the only space available), and lessons were taught by an educated young prisoner who had been convicted of stealing a watch. Many of the women prisoners, themselves illiterate, crowded at the doorway to take in the reading lessons.

In 1817 Fry founded a committee of Quaker women volunteers called the Association for the Improvement of Female Prisoners (prison work was considered a respectable charitable undertaking for well-off women in that era). Each day two members of the association would visit the prison to distribute clothing and to conduct Bible readings. Committee members also distributed pieces of cloth and thread, giving inmates the opportunity to sew and earn money. The Association raised money to hire a female resident caretaker to replace the male guards.

Fry convinced government authorities to separate the women prisoners according to age and seriousness of offense and to grant each prisoner more living space. She was less successful in saving condemned prisoners from the gallows. In

1818 Fry intervened, unsuccessfully, on behalf of a servant named Harriet Skelton. Her persistent appeals to a cabinet minister named Lord Sidmouth prompted him to proclaim about Fry, before the House of Commons, that she was "removing the dread of punishment in the criminal classes."

Works on behalf of exiled prisoners

Fry also took up the cause of women prisoners sent into exile. In the early 1800s it was a practice of the English government to transport some female prisoners to New South Wales, in the British territory of Australia. There the prisoners worked as indentured servants. Fry was horrified to see the convicts chained together and herded in open carts from the prisons to the seaport. Some of the prisoners were even carrying children. Once aboard the ships, the prisoners suffered from a lack of food and clothing.

Due to Fry's lobbying efforts, the practice of shackling the women on their way to the ships was stopped. And with the aid of the Association for the Improvement of Female Prisoners, Fry was able to supply the prisoners with food and clothing for their voyage.

Urges prison reform throughout England and abroad

In 1818 Fry traveled with her brother, John Joseph Gurney, throughout northern England and Scotland. The pair visited local prisons, studying the conditions under which inmates were held. After visiting a prison, Fry would make suggestions to local authorities for improvment. Among her suggestions were providing separate units for women and men, and for major and minor offenders; placing only female guards in women's units; discontinuing beatings and capital punishment; and providing prisoners with educational opportunities, health care, and job training.

Fry also organized local women's organizations, the members of which would continue to visit the prisons and press for reforms after Fry had moved on. The organizations later joined together as the British Ladies' Society for Promoting the Reformation of Female Prisoners. In 1819 Gurney published a record of the pair's trip titled *Notes on a Visit to Some of the Prisons in Scotland and the North of England in Company with Elizabeth Fry.*

Fry's efforts were not limited to the British Isles. Among the places she took her campaign for prison reform were Russia, France, and Prussia. In each of those nations Fry won promises of prison improvements from members of the royal families. Fry rose to a position of international prominence enjoyed by few women during that era.

Establishes homeless shelter in London

Fry extended her concern not only to prisoners but also to homeless people. She was particularly moved by the death of a homeless boy who froze on a doorstep in London in 1819. Through her efforts, a homeless shelter was established in London. There homeless people could receive a meal and a place to spend the night. Fry formed an organization of women that volunteered to staff the shelter and help homeless people find employment.

Fry also was concerned about conditions in institutions for the mentally ill, or insane asylums as they were called. Fry found that those institutions were hardly distinguishable from prisons. She advocated that asylum residents be treated with kindness and that steps be taken to restore residents' sense of dignity, including allowing them to wear their own clothes (as opposed to institutional uniforms) and feeding them at tables set with tablecloths and utensils.

Family sinks into poverty

In 1827 Fry published a book about her experience with prison reform, titled *Observations on the Visiting, Superintendence and Government of Female Prisoners.* That book marked an end to Fry's work with prisoners, because in the following year the Fry family's finances fell into disarray and Fry's husband declared bankruptcy. Without the financial backing of her husband, Fry was forced to spend less time doing reform work and more time at home taking care of her family. Fry continued her duties as a Quaker minister, however, and volunteered with social welfare organizations when she was able.

With Fry on the sidelines, a rival prison reform movement took hold. The new reformers argued that stricter laws and harsher punishments—such as those imposed in the United States's penal system—were needed to reduce crime. (Crime had been a growing problem in England since the start of the Industrial Revolution—the surge in technological and economic development that drew masses of people to the cities—in the mid-eighteenth century.) Fry's rivals prevailed in the British House of Commons, which in 1835 passed a Prison Act that sanctioned solitary confinement, hard labor, and other strict forms of punishment.

Fry retained her celebrity status abroad. She traveled to France in 1838 and Germany in 1841, at the invitation of the respective governments. In 1842 the king of Prussia visited Fry at her home. Fry died on October 12, 1845, in Ramsgate, England, and was buried in a Quaker cemetery on the eastern edge of London.

Two years after Fry's death, two of her daughters compiled her journals into a two-volume set titled *Memoir of the Life of Elizabeth Fry with Extracts from her Journal and Letters.*

Sources

Books
"Elizabeth Fry." *Historic World Leaders.* Detroit: Gale Research, Inc., 1994.

"Fry, Elizabeth." *The Dictionary of National Biography.* Vol. 7. Edited by Leslie Stephen and Sidney Lee. London, England: Oxford University Press, 1917–1996.

Kent, John. *Elizabeth Fry.* New York: Arco Publishing Company, 1963.

Whitney, Janet. *Elizabeth Fry: Quaker Heroine.* Boston: Little, Brown, & Company, 1936.

Articles
Anderson, George M. "Elizabeth Fry (1780–1845): Timeless Reformer." *America.* October 14, 1995: 22+.

Index

Illustrations are marked by (ill.).

Black Creek Village *2: 209.*
See also Love Canal
Black Expo *2: 279*
Black Hills, South Dakota
1: 34–35
Black Panther Party *1: 39, 63,
72–79, 131–32; 2: 349*
Black Panther, The 1: 73
Black Power movement *1: 130*
Black Power (poster) *1: 74 (ill.)*
Black Skin, White Masks 1: 175
Blackwell, Unita *1: 80 (ill.),
80–87*
*Blackwell v. Issaquena County
Board of Education 1: 85*
"Bloody Sunday," *2: 310–11*
*Blues Legacies and Black Feminism:
Gertrude "Ma" Rainey, Bessie
Smith, and Billie Holiday
1: 133*
Bolsheviks *3: 454*
Bombing *1: 130*
"Bombingham," *3: 510*
Borneo *3: 411–12*
Botha, P. W. *2: 342, 356*
Brightman, Lehman "Lee," *1: 3*
British Broadcasting Corporation
(BBC) *3: 588*
Brotherhood of Sleeping Car
Porters (BSCP) *3: 443*
Brown, Elaine *1: 79*
Brown, John *1: 88 (ill.),
88–95, 156*
Brown v. Board of Education 577
Bryant, Louise *3: 453–54*
BSCP. *See* Brotherhood of Sleeping
Car Porters (BSCP)
Bureau of Indian Affairs (BIA)
1: 36
Burgos-Debray, Elizabeth *2: 390*
Burma *3: 540*
*Burma and India: Some Aspects of
Intellectual Life under
Colonialism 3: 541*
Burns, Lucy *3: 429*
Burnum, Burnum *3: 414–15,
415 (ill.)*
Bus boycotts *2: 246–47, 306–7;
3: 447, 478–81*
Bush, George *3: 486*
BYNC. *See* Back of the Yards
Neighborhood Council
(BYNC)

C

California Proposition 187 *3: 504*
California Proposition 209 *3: 504*
CAM. *See* Catholic Action
Movement (CAM)
Cambridge, Battle of *3: 464*
Cambridge, Maryland *3: 458*
Cambridge, Treaty of *3: 462–63*
Camp David Accords *2: 324*
"Campaign to End Slums," *2: 311*
Canada *3: 561*
CAP. *See* Chicago Area Project
(CAP)
Capital 2: 376
Capone, Al *1: 11*
Carl von Ossietzky Medal for
Courage *1: 125*
Carmichael, Stokely *3: 529 (ill.)*
Carranza, Venustiano *3: 594*
Carter, Amy *2: 266*
Carter, Jimmy *2: 207, 265, 324;
3: 486*
Caste system *2: 197*
Castro, Fidel *1: 145; 2: 230–33,
233 (ill.); 3: 437, 580*
Castro, Raul *2: 230*
Catholic Action Movement
(CAM) *1: 180*
Catholic Church *1: 122. See also*
Irish Republican Army
Catholic Peace Fellowship *1: 67*
Catholic Worker 1: 138–39
Catholic Worker communal
farms *1: 139*
Catholic Worker houses *1: 139*
Catholic Worker movement
1: 141
CBNS. *See* Center for the Biology
of Natural Systems (CBNS)
CCHW. *See* Citizen's
Clearinghouse for Hazardous
Waste (CCHW)
Center for Health, Environment,
and Justice (CHEJ) *2: 210*
Center for Study of Responsive
Law (CSRL) *3: 400*
Center for the Biology of
Natural Systems (CBNS)
1: 115–16, 119
Central Committee of the
Communist League *2: 375*
Central Intelligence Agency (CIA)
1: 22; 2: 229, 233; 3: 424, 497

Horton, Myles *1:* 5, 182–83, 183
(ill.); *2:* 243–44
Hostages *2:* 282
House Committee on
UnAmerican Activities
(HUAC) *3:* 471
House, Jonah *1:* 70
Howe, Julia Ward *3:* 520
HUAC. *See* House Committee on
UnAmerican Activities
(HUAC)
Huerta, Dolores *1:* 98, 100 (ill.),
100–101
Huerta, Victoriano *3:* 594
Hull, Charles *1:* 3
Hull House *1:* 3–5, 8; *2:* 300, 302
Hunger strike *3:* 544

I

"I Have a Dream," *1:* 31; *2:* 309
I, Rigoberta Menchú 2: 390
IAF. *See* Industrial Areas
Foundation (IAF)
IAT. *See* Indians of All Tribes (IAT)
*If They Come in the Morning: Voices
of Resistance 1:* 133
IFS. *See* International Federation
of Settlements and
Neighborhoods Centers (IFS)
Illinois Labor Act *2:* 301
Immigration and Naturalization
Service (INS) *3:* 438–39
Independent Political Council
3: 442
Indian Appropriations Act (1871)
1: 36
Indian Independence movement
2: 198, 200
Indian National Congress *2:* 197
Indian Opinion 2: 195
Indian Reorganization Act (IRA)
3: 568
Indian Rights *1:* 195
Indians of All Tribes (IAT) *3:* 550
Indigenous Woman 3: 569
Indigenous Women's Network
(IWN) *2:* 319; *3:* 568–69
Industrial Areas Foundation (IAF)
1: 13, 15–16
Industrial League *1:* 50
Industrial Workers of the World
(IWW) *1:* 60; *2:* 251, 253–54;
3: 455

INS. *See* Immigration and
Naturalization Service (INS)
Internal Security Act *3:* 414
International Brigade *1:* 12
International Congress of
Women *1:* 7
International Federation of
Settlements and
Neighborhoods Centers
(IFS) *1:* 4
International Indian Treaty
Council *2:* 389–90
IRA. *See* Irish Republican Army
(IRA)
IRA. *See* Indian Reorganization
Act (IRA)
Ireland *1:* 121
Ireland, Patricia *2:* 269 (ill.),
269–76
Irish Republican Army (IRA)
1: 121–22. *See also* Catholic
Church
Israel *2:* 324
IWN. *See* Indigenous Women's
Network (IWN)
IWW. *See* Industrial Workers of
the World (IWW)

J

Jackson, Jesse *2:* 277 (ill.),
277–83, 278 (ill.)
Jara, Victor *1:* 20–21
Jefferson, Thomas *1:* 35
Jewish Defense League (JDL)
2: 326
JDL. *See* Jewish Defense
League (JDL)
Jim Crow laws *1:* 182; *2:* 243,
247–48; *3:* 458
Jingsheng, Wei *2:* 284 (ill.),
284–90
Job discrimination *3:* 444
Johnny Damas and Me 3: 556
Johnson, Lyndon B. *2:* 311;
3: 424, 448, 534
Jones, Mary Harris "Mother,"
2: 291 (ill.), **291–97**
Junta *1:* 24; *3:* 489–90

K

Kansas City Chiefs *3:* 555
Kelley, Florence *1:* 5; *2:* 298 (ill.),
290–304

N

Socioeconomic factors *1:* 12

Sojourner Truth Educational Excellence Award *1:* 163

Soldiers of Islam *3:* 406

Soledad brothers *1:* 132

Somoza Garcia, Anastasio *3:* 494–95, 495 (ill.), 498

Sons and Daughters of the Incarcerated (SADOI) *1:* 188–89

Sons of Temperance *3:* 518

Soon to be a Major Motion Picture *2:* 266

Sourani, Raji *2:* 328, 329 (ill.)

South Africa *2:* 352

South End house *1:* 4

Southern Christian Leadership Conference (SCLC) *1:* 49, 51, 53; *2:* 279, 307; *3:* 524

Soviet Union *2:* 224

Spanish Civil War (1936–39) *1:* 12, 28; *2:* 225; *3:* 470

Spartacus League *2:* 335

Spear of the Nation *2:* 355

Spider Women's Theater *3:* 570

Spinning wheel *2:* 198

Spirituality *2:* 383

Sproul Hall *3:* 502

Stanton, Elizabeth Cady *3:* **515–22**, 515 (ill.)

Stanton, Henry B. *3:* 516

Starr, Ellen G. *1:* 3

State Law and Order Restoration Council (SLORC) *3:* 543

Steal This Book *2:* 264

Stone, Lucy *3:* 428 (ill.), 520

Student Nonviolent Coordinating Committee (SNCC) *1:* 49, 52, 54, 67, 73, 82, 131; *2:* 237; *3:* 448, 458–59, 500, **523–30**

Students for a Democratic Society (SDS) *2:* 235, 237, 262; *3:* 531 (ill.), **531–38**, 535 (ill.)

Suffrage *1:* 137; *2:* 217; *3:* 427–29, 520

Superfund law *2:* 208

Supporters *3:* 544 (ill.)

Survival News *2:* 380

Suu Kyi, Aung San *2:* 391; *3:* 539 (ill.), **539–48**

Sweatshops *2:* 301

T

Temperance *3:* 518

Ten Most Wanted List *1:* 133

"Ten Point Program," *1:* 76–77

Teters, Charlene *3:* 554–55, 555 (ill.)

Theater *3:* 467, 570

They Call Us Dead Men: Reflections on Life and Conscience *1:* 68

Thirteenth Amendment *3:* 519

Thoreau, Henry David *1:* 94

Tiananmen Square *2:* 287

Toleration Act (1689) *1:* 29

Torture *1:* 46–47

Touré, Sekou *3:* 423

Toynbee Hall *1:* 3–4

Trail of Broken Treaties *1:* 36; *3:* 552

Treason *3:* 454–55

Trial of the Catonsville Nine, The *1:* 68

Triangle Shirtwaist Company *2:* 223

Trotsky, Leon *1:* 18

Troublemaker: One Man's Crusade against China's Cruelty *3:* 589

Trudell, John *1:* 35; *3:* 549 (ill.), **549–57**

Truman, Harry S. *3:* 444

Truth, Sojourner *1:* 91; *3:* 562–63, 563 (ill.)

Tubman, Harriet *1:* 91; *3:* 558 (ill.), **558–65**, 561 (ill.)

Tubman, John *3:* 560

Turner, Nat *1:* 152 (ill.)

Tutela Legal *3:* 488

Twenty years at Hull House *1:* 6

TWO. *See* Woodlawn Organization, The (TWO)

U

UA. *See* Urgent Action (UA) network

UFW. *See* United Farm Workers Union (UFW)

UGCC. *See* United Gold Coast Convention (UGCC)

UMW. *See* United Mine Workers (UMW)

Underground Railroad *1:* 89–90; *3:* 560–61

Union County Public Library *3:* 578